Hippie Kitchen

A Measurefree Vegetarian Cookbook

Jean Johnson

Seventy-Sixth Avenue Press
3524 NE 76th Avenue
Portland, Oregon 97213

Library of Congress Control Number 2008908748

Johnson, Jean, PhD, 1948—

Hippie kitchen: a measurefree vegetarian cookbook

Includes index.

Cookery (Vegetables and Fruits)
Cookery (American—History)
Food Habits (United States)

ISBN-13 978-0-9815271-1-6
ISBN-10 0-9815271-1-6

Table of Contents

Introduction

A hippie kitchen is more than a space. It's more than even a time. Like, wow man, a hippie kitchen is a state of mind.

As you'd expect, a hippie kitchen transcends the mainstream in Timothy Leary's best fashion. It's within a hippie kitchen that everyday vegetarian cooks turn on, tune in, and leave the small chemistry approach to cooking behind.

No more leveling off precise measurements like we're in some sort of science lab. No more letting the elite cooking authorities have all the fun. When we rock & roll in a hippie kitchen, we move beyond a paint-by-numbers approach to cooking.

Measurefree cooking seems radical, but it's simply a return to the way things were. Americans didn't have measuring cups or rely on formal recipe books a century ago. More, everyday ethnic cooks around the world have happily managed without measurements and step-by-step instructions for centuries upon centuries. To this day these cooks turn out excellent, rustic food easily, quickly, and affordably. Cooks in hippie kitchens can get their act together too.

Forty years have come and gone since Alice Waters' gourmet pal, George Keller, called the fledging whole foods meals of the Sixties "hippie crap." Since then the great vegetables and beautifully made food Waters and Keller revered has gained popularity. As it has, eating well has developed an elite cache—one not always in our better interests.

Consider that in 2007 an upscale Portland, Oregon, restaurant offered a half dozen radishes on the stem rolling around a mound of butter with coarse salt for $4—quite good, actually, except for bitter aftertaste of the price. "Spread the butter on the radishes as you eat them," the waiter informs the untutored. "Like the French do." Or this from David Kamp's *The United States of Arugula*: a small chain of avant garde Japanese restaurants in the US charges "$15 for edamame—the traditional cheapo premeal snack of salted fresh green soybeans—by serving the beans still attached to the branch."

No wonder Kamp takes on the gourmet food establishment in the closing remarks of his book: "The foodie sophisticates need to lose their smugness and patronizing tone," he writes even as he aims his lens at the opposite end of the American culinary spectrum as well. "The junk food and diet food people need to learn that natural and gourmet foods need not be flavorless."

Enter the hippie kitchen. Flower children may have boiled up pots of overspiced vegetables and gluey brown rice back in the good old daze amen, but four decades have come and gone since. The crunchy granolas—one of the friendlier monikers hippies earned—have managed to keep some of their original food cooperatives open and generally steer a course true to original intent: eating lower on the food chain and freeing themselves from weirded out plastic food. In the process, hipsters have not only improved their cooking, their ideas have percolated into mainstream culture.

Tofu, olive oil, and whole grains might have been nigh unto heresy back when drugs, sex, and rock & roll didn't exactly help hipster credibility. But now even those who regularly dose on burgers and fries have heard of, if not eaten and enjoyed, these affordable, healthy foods. More, many carnivores have the occasional meatless dinner, an approach to eating the straight establishment took serious umbrage over when counterculture types went vegetarian in the Sixties.

So food coming from hippie kitchens these days is the antithesis of what George Keller decried. It's superb food. Simple food that's mostly quick and inexpensive to make. That's because cooks in hippie kitchens have busy lives and budgets to keep in check. They want to cook for the new economy and save the 10 to 50 percent extra it costs to produce packaged food. They want to eat well and tighten their belts.

Cooks in hippie kitchens also wonder how formalized recipes ever got their grip on us in the first place. Why science was allowed to so easily bully the art of cooking into meek submission. These free spirits want to discover what the world's ethnic cooks have known for centuries: that it's immensely gratifying and generally great fun to pull together everyday food from what's on hand in a creative, intuitive way.

Free spirits in the kitchen. It's a transition whose time has come. A legacy to which we are entitled and one that has clear historical roots in global ethnic traditions.

I might not have appreciated this had I not lived a decade with the Hopi and Navajo in the Southwest.

Life in Hopiland and Navajoland taught me about taking a single foodstuff and building an entire cuisine around it. From the paper-thin piki bread of Hopi women like Alfreda Secakuku to the huge hand ground corn cake Navajo matriarchs like Shirley Begay bake in pits to celebrate their daughters' entry into womanhood, the people of the Four Corners have their corn cuisine down. Somiviki or blue marbles—little dumplings from finely ground blue corn—had to be my favorite at Joyce Tawayesva's where we sat around her Hopi table and dipped the dumplings into a central communal skillet of fried red chile.

When I went off to graduate school it was as if there was a gravitational pull—most likely set into motion well before my time in Indian country by my mother who loved Korean kimchi and prided herself on making big stinky batches of the spiced, pickled cabbage. Whatever the case, between my mother's adventurous cooking and my adventures, when I met Anju Bhatia the karma was right.

It was in Anju's kitchen that I discovered the centuries-old vegetarian cuisine of India. The smell of cumin seeds frying in hot oil. The cool yogurt Anju decorated with a crosshatching of ground coriander. The jarred lemon pickles full of spice that I started putting on everything including peanut butter sandwiches.

I also met Rula Awwad-Rafferty who carries the mystique of the Middle Eastern in her genes. Rula introduced me to a Ramadan feast—and not merely as a spectator.

Hummus. Tabbouleh. Baba ghanoush. We made it all. Rula tutored me in working parsley over. How to chop and mince, and mince and chop until the herb was an ultrafine dross. And garlic. We pounded it to "smithereens," as Rula put it, laughing over a glass of red wine. We smashed the garbanzo beans until they were perfectly, perfectly smooth. Nothing less would do in Rula's kitchen.

In all instances, there were no recipe books or measuring or packaged, processed foods. The cooking I did with Alfreda, Shirley, Joyce, Anju, and Rula was a creative calculus of adding enough water until the batter looked right or using enough garlic to make the home-cooked garbanzo beans we smashed into hummus taste good. It was cooking with good, honest food. It was cooking without measurements and stuffy directions.

Yes, it's true that by shunning processed food in gaudy packages and bottles, cooks in hippie kitchens spend more time slicing and dicing fresh produce, whisking up their own salad dressings, and steaming whole grains. My experience, though, is that once we free ourselves from formal recipes, we find hanging out in the kitchen cool—and discover not only ways to keep the mess under control but also streamline the task of making great everyday food. (See: On The Cook Counts Too & On Flash Cooking, pages 44 & 45.)

What was mindless drudgery turns into a groove. Instead of sorrow in our heart of hearts at having to follow orders from headquarters, we are empowered. Also, once we get a taste for freshly made food, we wonder why we ever chowed down on the spendy packaged stuff in the first place. Stuff that takes a toll on our bodies with its load of salt, sugar, flour, and so-called natural flavor brewed up in chemistry labs to give food well beyond its prime something we call shelf life.

Getting a hippie kitchen organized for real cooking is not particularly demanding. My scene has a broom handy for sweeping up and a great big chopping board for slicing and dicing. And over the years a family of cast iron vessels— wok, griddle, and a couple skillets—have appeared, making washing pots and pans almost obsolete. Between those and a chef's knife, box grater, blender, paring knife, and handy-dandy pastry scraper for scooping things up, I have a happening scene. I'm in business.

In business. Sounds a bit odd describing a lefty hippie kitchen. Business has conservative connotations, as in mass production and profits. Conservatives, though, are about more than making money. They are also about local control, about community. So it's in this latter respect that the business of a hippie kitchen intersects with conservative ideas.

John Schwenkler makes precisely that case in "Food for Thought," an article published in the June 2008 issue of *The American Conservative*. A doctoral student in philosophy at UC Berkeley at the time, Schwenkler argued that "renewing the culinary culture should be a conservative cause" because it promotes "real local autonomy that is not undermined by corporate agribusiness." This change, he maintained, "will have to take root in our kitchens first."

Right on, bro! We're only too happy to welcome conservatives into our hippie kitchens. We hipsters have spent four decades paving the way down the rockier parts on the path, building bridges over many troubled waters. Sixties hippies long ago identified the Standard American Diet (SAD) and the corporations that get people strung out on strange food, as a major bummer.

But we liberals aren't covetous. We know, like our new president, Barack Obama, that if we want to make true headway on resolving issues, we need to dialogue not dictate. So we say, welcome to our culinary counterculture. Welcome to the world of farmers markets and family farms where animals are truly husbanded like they were before efficient factory farming started treated them like mere machines. Welcome to buying local and growing your own without chemicals like Michelle Obama is doing at the White House. Welcome to cooking up great food without putting on a pair of reading glasses to follow some tight-laced set of prescriptive instructions.

Besides, in hippie kitchens we don't much mind whether the person coming through the door with fresh, local produce and a yen for a good meal is liberal or conservative. That's because it's over first rate food that conversation can begin. It's riffing around the world of sustainability that an ethical food consciousness can arise. And it's in connecting with the age old artistry of cooking that this down home, delicious revolution turns into funky friggin' groove.

Jean Johnson
Portland, Oregon
June 2009

Spring Eats

Spring. You don't have to remember Hair and be hung up on the Age of Aquarius to want to "let the sun shine in," or a Beatles fan to know that after "a long, cold, lonely winter," the returning yellow orb is out of sight. Spring is that quickening time of year. A time when in Procol Harum's words, we want to "skip the light fandango and turn cartwheels cross the floor."

Yet it takes time to catch an authentic spring buzz. New life, bright green shoots, can't be rushed. First come the teasers. Chives with the equinox. Not far behind, the famous quartet—parsley, sage, rosemary, and thyme. Our appetites are whetted. We yearn for the snow peas of June if not the tomatoes of August. But in her wisdom, Mother Nature holds the bar steady. "Patience my dears," she seems to say, "In due time."

So we slog through more showers. We watch the first snow drops and daffodils and tulips bloom. We breathe deep the sweet perfume of hyacinths—all the while leaning on lemons to keep our gratitude going for cabbages and parsnips and winter squashes. Finally, though, the goddesses have mercy. The earth begins to warm, and Donovan's "sunshine comes softly" through our kitchen windows. Asparagus stalks through our doors with the bold assurance of a welcoming kiss. Then a tumble of offerings appear: spinach, fresh green garlic, fava beans, slender green onions, radishes, fennel, watercress, morel mushrooms, peas, rhubarb, new potatoes, strawberries, not to mention the California treats: avocados, artichokes, and early apricots. There are even pineapples in their prime from Hawaii and high quality mangoes from Florida. If that's not enough for America's immense seasonal bounty, fresh mint and winter savory deck our garden paths alongside dainty red coral bells.

Spring eats. Time to play-play.

Spring Eats

Spaghetti Squash Primavera (aka Hippie Hash)

Not the kind of gonzo hash that flower children got high on during the Summer of Love but certainly good grub. All it takes is leftover spaghetti squash and whatever spring veggies are handy. The point is to jive with what the moment offers.

Recipe Note

Flash cook green garlic on high in a heavy pan with a little oil (page 45). Splash in a puddle of water and fluff in some leftover spaghetti squash to warm with the garlic. At the very end, in goes a chop of spinach which wilts nicely and quickly. Dress simply with oil, red wine vinegar, salt, pepper, chives, and if you want to make cornmeal waffles, check out page 130.

Details

Per usual, if I'd had lemons on hand, I wouldn't have picked up the vinegar bottle. Then again, red wine vinegar never disappoints and did its chore of lifting the flavors. I could even have used plain white or cider vinegar, jugs of which are always handy in my thrifty hippie pantry.

On Primavera—

In Italian, primavera means in the style of spring. So classic pasta primavera has young spring veggies either left raw or flash cooked (page 45).

On Eating Winter Squash in Spring—

We all know what happens when we take things too literally— when we put too fine a point on ideas. So there's no need to freak out and object to winter squash in spring.

If you think about it, given that the earth is only beginning to warm enough to produce new green life, we're lucky to have good keepers like the hard shell squashes to help tide us over. Besides, spaghetti squash is a healthy change from pasta. So do one better than hugging a winter squash today. Stick that great big beautiful honey in the oven and bake it up nice and hot.

On a New Potato Roll with Primavera—

A bunch of flash cooked asparagus (page 40) cut into little logs and a bouquet of chopped flat leaf parsley combine with delicate steamed new potatoes for this round. A pat of butter and thin shavings of Parmigiano-Reggiano give this primavera remarkably good vibrations.

On the Parmesan Cheese Family—

Wedges of parmesan are so user friendly, there's no need to buy the cheese already grated. Yet, as my father huffed when I hassled my mother for using the pre-grated stuff in her Caesar salads, "That little green can was good all those years."

It's nice to grate or dice official Parmigiano-Reggiano from Italy over food when it can star. More often, though, when you want the salty tang the parmesan cheese family brings, a more affordable domestic parmesan works. It's the same with Asiago and Romano. The Italians have it down, but the domestics cost less. A way to see what you think is to buy some wedges and test them out. (Also see page 28.)

On Green Garlic—

Mild spring garlic is a cook's delight since the papery husks that normally encase each clove are still succulent and can be minced right up with the flesh—as the photograph shows.

You'll find green garlic at farmers markets in various sizes from small ones reminiscent of scallions to those that are starting to develop proper garlic heads. Besides being a dream to work with, green garlic is mild as a lamb.

On Cheese & the Cows that Make It Happen—

The lady cows do appreciate us watching for cheeses made from milk produced by dairy farmers that truly husband their herds. We consumers have power here. Collectively, we really do. We can use our milk money to rescue bossies from factory farms gone awry. Rescue cows with their thousand-pound frames from hours on unforgiving cement floors. We can help get the cows back out into green pastures to chew their cud and switch their tails.

Primavera Frittata

There's no reason a primavera can't become an eggy frittata—or that radishes can't be flash cooked, turning into altogether different creatures. The focaccia that's pictured was fun too and matched the frittata wedge for wedge. Check out a version of this popular Italian yeast bread on page 152. You'll find that breads don't need to be made exclusively from flour and how easily focaccia morphs into pizza pie.

Recipe Note

Whisk up some eggs with a little water to help them bind and fold in cheese and a chop of flash cooked veggies (page 45). In this case I used radishes, asparagus, and kale flash cooked in that order. They cooled enough to add to the eggs while I was dicing the Monterrey Jack and crumbling up the blue cheese. The works went into an oiled cast iron skillet and medium oven until the eggs were set. The hot wedges were great, as were the cold ones the next day.

Dolores' Dipped Strawberries

My family's style with strawberries is pretty traditional: usually shortcake, jams, or just pulled apart when they are perfectly ripe from Oregon's cherished spring crop. But when Laura Berg— HH's keeper (page 36)—returned from her nephew Shane's high school graduation with tales of strawberries dipped in dark chocolate that her mother did, I listened up. Mrs. Berg is a member of the old guard but many of her nine children came of age during the Sixties scene. Besides Dolores' Dipped Strawberries transcend time and space and thus fully qualify in a hippie kitchen.

Recipe Note

Melt dark and white chocolate in separate heavy bottomed pans. Cut the tips off the ends of the berries, twirl the fruit in the chocolate, and chill.

Details

My store sells dark chocolate chunks in the bulk bins. I also nabbed some white chocolate chips to give those a try. From there it was warming the chocolate in small pots on the stove and trimming off the tiny tip ends like Dolores did so the berries sit upright. Then simply a dip and swish with the berries.

The dark chocolate was easier to work with than the white chips. I suspect the chips aren't pure chocolate and whatever they're adulterated with made them a little thick once they were melted, not as spready and glossy as the dark chocolate was.

Laura said she and her mom liked the berries best chilled, so that's what I did. Set them on wax paper on a plate and put them in the icebox. Then after dinner, out they came. It was worth the wait. Every single one of those puppies went down like elixir from the goddesses.

Thank you Mrs. Berg; your touch shows. Your steady touch as a great scratch cook all those years when you were raising your many children. Your touch as a kitchen gardener, no matter the short growing season of your Montana home. And now, your whimsical touch as the matriarch of the family celebrating a grandchild coming of age.

Asparagus-Cheese Toasts

This brunchy sandwich puts a trendy spin on grilled cheese. You can make these toasts open face to show off the gus as pictured, or go for the traditional two-slices-of-bread approach. I used a chèvre here, but if you don't speak goat cheese and don't want to, try Monterrey Jack, ricotta, fontina, or even cheddar.

Recipe Note

Flash cook some skinny asparagus in lengths to fit your toast (page 45) and bring a griddle or heavy skillet up to medium heat. Dot some bread with butter or brush it with olive oil and grill both sides if you're doing an open face sandwich.

Layer the cheese on the toasted bread and sprinkle with lemon zest—or actually work the zest into the cheese if you're using a chèvre or ricotta.

Turn the heat down low, top with a lid, and wait a couple minutes for the cheese to get yummy. Angle your asparagus across the top. Dress with a squeeze of lemon juice. Garnish with a bit more of the wonderfully aromatic zest.

On Flavor—

Scientists say much of what we perceive as taste is actually picked up by our highly sophisticated olfactory apparatus in our nose and back of the mouth. Inhale and see what you think.

On a Roll with Asparagus—

Some millet risotto's not half bad with flash cooked asparagus. Toast the millet in oil. Add a slug of white wine and cook that off before starting the boiling and stirring routine with vegetable broth made from a strained infusion of boiled carrots, celery, onion, and parsley (page 164). Once the millet is creamy, dose it with butter and parmesan before stirring in bite sized pieces of flash cooked asparagus, reserving the prettiest tips for the top.

On Meyer Lemons—

It's hard to overstate the appeal of fresh lemon—especially if you treat yourself to a thin-skinned, canary yellow Meyer lemon. Meyers are sweeter than the run of the mill because they're a cross between an orange and a lemon that a Californian named Meyer brought from China a century ago. Whatever kind of fresh lemons you work with, you'll appreciate how they lift the flavor of all kinds of food. Indeed, the story goes that there's not much five star chefs don't put lemon juice in—including a few secret drops in mashed potatoes.

Introducing HH

Spring and lovers seem to go together, so no season like the present to introduce HH. He lives with friend Laura Berg and was quick to spot Celeste on the back cover of the first volume in this measurefree cookbook trilogy. Life has not been the same since for Mr. HH.

At first Celeste received his overtures with interest. After all it's not every woman who lounges around with her big belly boldly displayed who receives the attentions of a dapper gentleman. She gave his first froggy went a courtin' email more than just a glance and seemed impressed with the photo he attached.

But last fall when HH started croaking about meeting in person, Celeste turned her very lovely back on him. We're not sure if it was the time of year or what. In any event, once winter was on the wane and HH's bug eyes broke the surface of the water once again, Celeste had apparently thought it over.

She sniffed as to how she guessed it was okay for him to make an appearance here in the pages of *Hippie Kitchen*—just as long as the back cover was

100 percent,
exclusively,
hers.

Mango Mint Ice

Here's a way to swirl young spring spearmint and mango into an icy treat. Either drink it pronto or hold it over in the freezer, letting it stand out a good half hour before you serve.

Recipe Note

Blend fresh mango, sugar, and spearmint leaves in a blender until smooth. Add enough chile flakes and lime juice to get your attention. Then some ice to render this concoction oh so cold and fabulous—whether you drink it like a smoothie or spoon it up like an icy sorbet.

Details

Add a little sugar and a few spearmint leaves (that have a flavor preferable to most peppermints) at a time until you've got a taste that appeals. (Or see page 114 on muddling.) A good three limes will stand up to a single mango, depending on how juicy they are and how big the mango is. That's because the sour element really needs to be there to send this drink over the top.

On the chile flakes, tasting your way is the key. Too little and your brew lacks spunk. Too much and the heat dominates more than your mother would think proper.

Sometimes I add rhubarb simmered in white wine to the mint instead of mango. Between the tart note of the rhubarb and the winey nuances, expect an usually interesting undertone.

Flash Cooked Asparagus

It's spring and even Portlanders normally not into the NBA are talking about the Blazer's valiant season and effort to stay alive in the 2009 playoffs. What to do but gather around the tube and watch the game with friends. We nabbed an pizza from Lucca's, a local hand crafter with a brick oven that decorates the crust with things like wood-roasted wild mushrooms, fontina, mozzarella, parsley, and truffle oil. To go with, a quick salad and flash cooked asparagus, projects that took only minutes so we wouldn't miss tip off.

Recipe Note

Put a skillet or wok on high heat with a good pour of water. Snap the tough ends of your asparagus off and put the spears in the skillet. Splash in more water now and then to keep the moisture going while the gus cooks. The goal is to wind up with tender asparagus just as the last of the water evaporates (page 45). If you have water left, though, and drink the lovely broth, you'll make a discovery you'll most likely adore. When the end of one of your thicker stalks is soft to the tip of a paring knife, cut the heat, and dress your gorgeous green spears with olive oil, fresh lemon juice, salt, and a grind of black (or white) pepper.

Details

When you snap the ends of asparagus off instead of cutting them, the stalks will break at the point where they are tender, thus eliminating tough ends. If you can't live with the edges being a little ragged trim them up with a knife.

More Details

Some chefs and home cooks don't like to break the ends off asparagus. Instead they trim away the tough peeling from the edible inner part. That's certainly an approach, although one that makes working with asparagus reminiscent of getting potatoes ready for the pot. If you want another idea on not wasting the ends of the stalks, save them for cream of asparagus soup. There's even an easy vegan version.

Flash cook the asparagus ends with onion, unpeeled grated potatoes, a nice pour of white wine, and enough water to keep things cruising. Season with salt and pepper. Once the vegetables are done, put the works through a ricer or into a blender. (If you go the blender route and are working with vegetables and broth hot from the stove, it's mandatory to take precautions so you don't get burned. Fill the blender half way only. Then fold a thick kitchen towel or two and hold the cloth firmly into place atop the blender lid before you flick the switch.)

The above approach to cream of asparagus soup relies on potatoes to thicken the broth. You can bolster this lean version by stirring in some cream if you like. Or you can leave out the potatoes entirely and revel in the rich dairy scene, even making a roux (paste in French) by combining equal parts flour and butter—two tablespoons thickens a cup of liquid—over medium heat and then whisking in milk or cream and seasoning with salt and pepper.

But back to flash cooked asparagus. Besides being an ultrafast method, the beauty of this approach is that your spears don't lose their righteous color. I should know. Back in the days when I thought cooking vegetables meant putting them in a pot of water with a lid, I turned my share of asparagus—not to mention peas and broccoli an unpleasant color. Even after I graduated to using steamer baskets that preserved nutrition by keeping the veggies out of the water, I somehow didn't make the connection between the weird color and the almighty lid. I mean, if a pot has a lid it means you're supposed to use it. No?

Yet, even after I understood that lids worked best for steaming rice and carrots, I was light years from figuring out the beauty of flash cooking. Rather I marveled at the asparagus my aunt produced by just pressing a number on her microwave. Soon I was the proud owner of my own magic box, and my asparagus came out green, just like auntie's. There was a problem, though. My kitchen is small, and the micro dominated a whole corner. Through the years I developed a dislike of the big establishment box—so much so that when it finally gave up the ghost, I resigned from the microwave clan.

That was how I ended up backing into the door of flash cooking (page 45). It took some time, but the draw was irresistible. No lids. No zapping in the microwave. And certainly none of that taking things like asparagus off the heat and plunging them into ice water baths to stop the cooking instantaneously like you're in some sort of chemistry lab.

Flash cooking. Just a common sense approach to getting vegetables on the table easily and quickly with their beauty and health in full flower. It's a way someone like me who's busy at work all day can approach making good food. An affordable, low-tech, ultrafast way of cooking. A way I hope you find as easy and fun as I have.

On the Cook Counts Too—

Fussing with cooking vegetables by the singleton is something I do less often than not. That's because when you're going for a quick meal, it's easier to get a bunch of veggies onto the heat to flash cook together, warm salad or soup style. Between that and leftover grain and protein waiting in the fridge, you're there.

The singleton scene could be that's why so many of us spend forever in the kitchen—sometimes resenting the time and trouble. We think we have to make picture perfect meals every day with these separate little piles of whatever.

Contrast that with the spirit of one-bowl meals popular around the world. Ethnic cooks from Asia to Latin America to Africa know how to combine an enticing array of vegetables, fruits, grains, and legumes into easy meals. They know that the cook's happier and the food's better when they keep things simple.

It's the same thing on how much of this and that to put into what you're making. The cook needs to count. The cook does count. It's the cook's call.

That's why one day when journalist, Laura Marble who took to measurefree cooking instantly, asked how many tomatoes I knew to put in some dish or other, I came back with a reply that made us chuckle. "I don't know?" I said gearing up for a flip but seriously radical remark. "Like when I'm tired of chopping."

On Flash Cooking—

My Dad called me "High Heat Johnson." He had me pegged and knew I took after my mother. Mom's friends said she couldn't even spell the word patience.

So I come to flash cooking honestly. When I cruise into the kitchen I want stuff done now. I want to pull leftover grains and legumes from the icebox and spin them together with a bunch of vegetables pronto. So I turn the heat up full blast and go for it. I used to think this tendency an indolent cop out, but after traveling in other countries, I discovered that I'm not the only one flash cooking and that there's not a thing in the universe wrong with this approach to food.

To flash cook vegetables, start with a puddle of water, spices if you're in the mood, and high heat. The idea is to use just enough water to cook your vegetables, adding small pours as you go—making sure to get things that take the longest to cook in the pot first.

My favorite vehicle by far for flash cooking is a cast iron wok because it holds the heat so beautifully and turns the vegetables crisp tender in minutes. But as I've discovered cooking in other

As well known chef and restaurant owner, Rick Bayless, told the *New York Times Magazine* in response to a question about the biggest mistake home cooks make:

"They don't cook over high enough heat, and they don't salt enough."

I'd add that a benefit of high heat is that you don't have to wait around on dinner. It's done in a flash.

people's kitchens, regular woks, heavy bottomed skillets, and generally any pot or pan rattling around in the cupboard will be your friend.

It is true that flash cooking is an Asian stir fry in spirit since there's lots of vegetables and full blast heat. But that's where the similarities end. That's because flash cooking isn't bound by a particular orchestration of bok choy, soy sauce, and their buddies. Instead flash cooked dishes are free to move about in the world of fusion cuisine.

Flash cooked dishes can also skip the heat entirely and use raw vegetables. So in truth, the idea behind flash cooking is more about the flash and less about the heat. It's also a way cooks in hippie kitchens get to muster all the soul at their command and sketch out flavors that appeal in a thousand different hues.

So, get all those blues. Must be a thousand hues.
And be just differently used. You just know.
You sit there mesmerized.
By the depth of those eyes that you can't categorize.
She got soul. She got soul. She got soul!

~Bluebird, Buffalo Springfield, 1966

You got soul?

Mesmerized?

Far out...

A Zesty Experience—

When zesting, it's all a matter of holding the lemon in your left hand and turning it as you run the microplane (rasp) over the skin. That way you capture the fragrant yellow veneer, avoiding the bitter pith just below the surface.

Consider investing in a microplane if you don't have one. These tools come in large and small sizes and make zesting so easy you'll really get into the habit.

A large rasp is great for citrus and parmesans, while the petite critter pictured does fresh nutmeg proud.

Grandma-GK's Rhubarb Pie

There's the clump of rhubarb Grandma planted out back. Then there's decades listening to Prairie Home Companion's Garrison Keillor talk about how "Beebop-a-Rebop Rhubarb Pie takes the taste of humiliation out of your mouth." Between Grandma and Beebop-a-Rebop, I had to give a nod to the institution of rhubarb pie.

Recipe Note

Use two parts flour to one part fat for your crust. In this case, I used two cups of unbleached white flour (departing from my usual whole wheat pastry flour) and two or three pinches of salt to two cubes of cold butter pared off in thin bits with a knife. That way the butter is fairly easy to work into the flour by pressing the bits flat with your fingers. Then little splashes of ice water, using your hands to help the dough come together gently. Most recipes call for glass, nonreactive pie plates for rhubarb, so I used one, although as you can see, I set it in a giant cast iron pan to help the cause of getting the bottom done.

A couple pounds of chopped rhubarb—or enough to mound nicely into one large pie shell—takes a little less than a cup and a half of sugar and around a third cup of thickening like tapioca flour or just regular flour. A nonreactive bowl here really does keep the rhubarb from darkening, something I'm not sure is necessary with the pie plate given the crust as a go-between. In any event, off to the land of spices. I used allspice that I ground fresh in the coffee grinder. And once I got the lattice on and painted with a wash to make it shine—an egg white whisked with a little water—I sprinkled more allspice on the crust as well.

Bake your pie in a hot, 425 degree oven for ten minutes to jump start the bottom crust. Then back the heat off a good hundred degrees for a slow cook on the fruit and the top crust. Check your pie fairly often and turn it, since if your oven's like mine it's hotter at the back. Pies are done when the tip of your sharp knife signals soft fruit within.

Details

When I worked at My Mom's Pie shop way back, I'd make pies during my off hours and take wedges into the owner, Jean McLaughlin. Her main tip was to not get up tight about working the fat into the flour perfectly. And I did find that my crusts got flakier when I didn't worry about the little pea-sized bits. I got two thumbs up from Jean too, who wondered if I was planning on opening my own shop. I went to grad school instead, but I kept up with the pies, even learning to flatten the rim of the crimped crust so it doesn't burn.

Morels in Garlic Butter

It was years ago in Eastern Oregon when friends fresh in from anthropological work in the forest invited me over for my first morel mushrooms. "We were in a burned over area," Jan and Fred Jaehnig explained, flicking some char off one of the larger morels and tossing it into a sizzle of garlic butter along with the others. "That's often where you find these."

Within minutes the wild mushrooms were done. Jan spread a white cloth on the lunch table, and Fred poured white wine into tumblers. They passed a crusty white baguette, perfect for sopping up the earthy juices of the meaty morels. So simple, yet unforgettable; one of the better meals of my life. Jan and Fred—here's to you.

Recipe Note

Cut your larger morels in half and soak in salt water overnight or at least for a few hours. Then rinse well to remove debris from the crevices. You can skip this step, as I have on occasion, but if you do there will inevitably be a little grit left to remind you of the forest floor from whence your delicacies came.

Melt plenty of butter and add your shrooms and minced garlic, sautéing until the mushrooms are tender—which ideally is when the garlic is crispy and browned. Pour the wine, pass the bread, and let your consciousness expand.

Fava Bean Sass

Between not double peeling the beans and the homemade peanut sauce that goes with, this sass has turned into an annual affair. But unlike the garden sass that early New Englanders ate, Fava Bean Sass doesn't accompany, it takes the limelight.

Recipe Note

Flash cook fava beans and peapods on high heat (page 45). Dress with Tripped Out Peanut Sauce (page 56) and garnish with a chop of roasted peanuts from the organic bulk bins.

Details

As far as ratios and amounts go it depends on what you have in the house. I used one part favas shucked from their large pods to three parts peapods. I also opted for a change of pace on whole peapods and sliced them thinly on the diagonal, something that made this dish sassy indeed.

Into my cast iron wok on a high burner went the favas and peapods with a few splashes of water. It only took a two or three minutes for the favas to turn into tender, pale green lima bean look alikes. That's flash cooking for you.

I suppose a person could double peel the outer shell encasing each fava bean the way so many American cookbooks insist, but I followed the lead of Mediterraneans who are better acquainted with these early broad beans. As the picture of fresh favas nestled into their velvety pods shows, there's nothing about them that demands double peeling. That said, once they are flash cooked the husk turns a milky color in fairly short order. So you'll have to make your own call here, remembering that we're talking everyday food not fancy restaurant fare.

One thing's for certain, double peeling favas is something that stops many of us from messing with them. So if you simply can't eat the favas like they come, you might think unpitted olives and let everyone do their own at the table. We've tried that with older favas in which the husk really does get too tough to enjoy, and it was cool.

It's amazing what a tiny bit of garnish does to make food look so good you feel like torching up the old lava lamp for the dinner hour. You always can count on nuts for their appeal, or take another direction with this sass and try a chop of fresh spearmint.

On a Roll with Fava Beans—

This dish was such a pleasure to make and eat I could hardly wait for another dinner to roll around. Plus there was plenty of peanut sauce waiting in the fridge with more shelled favas. As far as the peapods, they were proliferating like rabbits out on the vines.

Round 1—Favas & Raisins

Leftover millet from the morning's breakfast joined flash

On Sass—

Like their counterparts in Britain, early New Englanders thought of vegetables merely as sauces to accompany meats.

They commonly referred to them as "garden sass," writes historian Harvey Levenstein in *Revolution at the Table.*

cooked favas and peapods with raisins and chopped radishes added at the last minute to preserve their cheery red color. For liquid, I used the end of the morning's pot of mint tea instead of plain water. This is a great trick born of a frugal eye. On this round, instead of the precise little diagonals I troubled over the first time with the peapods, I reverted to the standard rustic chop that's such an ultrafast way to ready veggies for the pot. I changed the ratio as well because there were plenty of favas left in the fridge and I didn't feel like going out to pick more peapods. Half and half it was.

Also since the peanut sauce was already made, I could use my time for assessing its flavor. The spicy heat was fine if not a bit over the top, something to remember to tone down next time. On sweetness, the raisins were a hit. The other half of the sweet-spicy-sour-salty quartet, though, needed a boost. I went for another pinch or two of coarse salt and then a conservative splash of sherry vinegar that was sitting out handy. Blend and taste again. So totally stunning the difference from just a lace of acid and perfecting the salt. One would have thought to call it good, but I couldn't resist more raisins and peanuts. Then to tame the heat a bit, a dollop of plain yogurt. Some entirely excellent slumgullion, as my Iowa-bred mother would say—although in defense of so many ingredients, I was actually mimicking an Indian curry.

Round 2—Blue Cheese-Fava Tostada

No more peapods picked, but still several handfuls of favas that needed using. So I put them in the wok on high to flash cook with spring onions and fresh green garlic. This brew spooned beautifully onto warmed corn tortillas and brought enough heat to melt a crumble of blue cheese. Totally superior food.

Tripped Out Peanut Sauce

Peanut sauce is like pesto and Mexican mole; there are as many ways to approach it as there are cooks in the kitchen. You can stir it up from peanut powder sold by Asian grocers. You can whisk it up from a can of coconut milk and peanut butter.

Thrifty scratch cooks, though, might appreciate this Indonesian technique adapted from SJ Fretz's Vegetables—Dishes from Around the World *(1991). Then again, I might be partial to this approach because my meat-and-potatoes father was thoughtful enough to give me Fretz's slim calligraphied volume.*

Recipe Note

Flash cook cumin seeds, half an onion, grated apple, minced garlic, and grated carrot in a dab of oil, splashing in water to keep things from sticking (page 45). Sprinkle in pinches of coriander, turmeric, salt, and cayenne pepper, and take your pan off the heat. Fold in peanut butter and fresh lime juice. Use water or apple juice to thin the sauce down if need be.

No worries about getting things perfect or making mistakes. This is your Tripped Out Peanut Sauce. If you, in George Harrison's immortal words, "let it roll for all it's worth," you'll soon find your stride—find just the blend that echoes for you and yours.

"Let it roll. Let it roll. Let it roll. Let it roll. Let it roll. Let it roll."

Details

The theory behind peanut sauce is to create a spoonable concoction that balances salt, sweet, spice, and sour. If you want a point of departure on the pb, try a half cup for every apple.

You can use most any type of sour from lime juice to cider vinegar, going easy and tasting your way to perfection. It's the same with the fruit—anything to sweeten the pot will do: apples, grapes, pears, raisins, fat Medjool dates, fresh orange juice. The aromatics? Leave them out entirely or mix and match depending on what you have. The peanut sauce I made in early June had lots of fresh green garlic bulbs and no onions at all. Three heads of the young garlic worked fine. It was a purple variety and quite mild.

On Cleanup and Storage—

One way I streamline my cleanup is stash bowls of leftovers in the refrigerator with a plate over the top. Then again, if I'm out of small plates, one bowl inverted over another works too. Not only does this eliminate digging around in the plastic carton bin, it makes for easy access that can lead to nifty experiments.

In the case of peanut sauce, it might mean you're more inclined to spoon some onto plain yogurt then next time you have the munchies. I can vouch; the combo's no slouchy deal. Kind of sweet, peanutty, a little spicy with a sour hit—way more interesting than plain fruit and sugar ever thought of being.

On Getting Sauced—

If you're trying to work with seasonal produce, you'll discover that early spring isn't all it's cracked up to be when it comes to eats.

That's why some of the tribes call it the starving time of year. Still, it's amazing how a few tweaks with sauces can turn ho-hum food into dishes that get a second glance.

Take peanut sauce and snow peas. Usually we think of snow peas done up with the Asian flavors—soy sauce, ginger, garlic. But when you try something dense and sweet like peanut sauce, snow peas suddenly become a different, exceedingly compelling breed of cat.

So, have a blast getting your vegetables sauced. There's a zillion ways including just sticking nuggets of your favorite cheese down into hot vegetables or whizzing up almonds, a tad of water, and salt in the blender. Then again, there's the light, clean approach of oil and vinegar—or oil and fresh lemon or lime juice. Between that classic duo and good old salt and pepper, it's easy and fast to turn out food that's turned on.

On Getting Herbed—

There are so many kinds of herbs besides the one that President Bill Clinton didn't inhale. If you get some going outside the kitchen door or in pots in the window, you'll be glad you did. That is because herbs are like candlelight; they bring a lot of mood.

Without a vegetable in the house, a quick chop and scatter of summer savory, chives, thyme, rosemary, sage, or the old stand-by parsley is all it takes. Use herbs singly or together in one riotously rebellious mix—and take solace that at least most of them are legal in this nation of ours.

Kristy's Guacamole

Kristy Anderson's version of this classic deserves ink here because her grandmother, Vera Velasquez, had a Mexican food restaurant in Nogales. Kristy's family also has deep roots in the ranch country of southern Arizona. The family got a land grant way back when from none other than the King of Spain.

Recipe Note

Mash an avocado with sliced green onions, chopped tomato, diced green chiles, and salt. Open a bag of your favorite chips, and, as Kristy says, "Eat it all up!"

Details

Kristy uses creamy Haas avocados and doesn't "mash them to death" because she likes her guacamole chunky. She lightly folds in her Anaheim chiles and tomatoes as well, so they retain their shape and distinctiveness. Kristy aims for enough green onions, tomatoes, and green chile so that each bite is enlivened by the trio. Still not sure? Here's her comment: "I eyeball it. I taste it. If it's good, I eat it all up!"

There's no lemon or lime juice in Kristy's Guacamole because she doesn't appreciate the sour accents interfering with the richness of the avocado. "That's why I say to eat it all up. If you do—and if you make it right before you eat—the avocado won't have time to turn dark."

More Details

Although Kristy uses canned chiles these days, she knows how to roast green chile with the best of them. "I learned from Grandma and Mom and her sisters. But usually when I'm just making up some guacamole, I'm hungry and don't want to mess with all that."

We can all relate to not wanting to stop and roast chiles when we're getting a quick batch of guacamole out. Still Kristy did observe that one of the last cans of green chile she bought was watery, and foodie pundits far and wide tell us we forfeit flavor when we go for the convenience of processed food.

To get around the corporate canned scene, I put up my own green chile during harvest just like my late friend from Williams, Arizona, Juanita Baca, used to do. It's easy to roast Anaheims on a tray in the oven. You turn them once so they blister on both sides. Then you can pull the skins off and the core of hot seeds out. A half dozen at a time slipped into little baggies for the freezer can be quite welcome in the dead of winter.

Kristy may not be a purist when it comes to her green chile, but she is about adding other niceties to guacamole. In her view, the avie-onion-tomato-chile-salt quintet is the only happening scene in the Southwest. So if you want to impress Ms. Anderson the next time you venture over to her hacienda for a *cerveza* or Margarita, bring the traditional dip not some gussied up nouvelle cuisine version. "I know people add garlic and cumin and things like that, but I like my guacamole this way."

On a Roll with Avocados—

Vegans know avocados as their butter and meat. India's revered Mahatma Gandhi knew them as superior food that rescued his body from the fasts he undertook on behalf of Indian independence in the 1940s.

Avies are great smashed up for guacamole, layered into in a whole wheat sandwich with alfalfa sprouts, slivered atop a green salad with grapefruit sections and red onion, or all duded up with sour cream and green onions for saucing pasta.

The neighborhood noodle shop around the corner, however, says to heck with all that. The Vietnamese people who run the place just plop half an avocado in a blender, add milk and sugar, and hit the button. This drink is way delightful alongside one of their Vietnamese pancakes. Yet for a creative measurefree cook, it's more of an invitation than a done deal.

When at home I fiddle, blending in ice cubes to turn the drink super cold and icy. It's also nice to squeeze off the juice from a whole lemon into the blender, a trick that gives this smoothie some serious legs.

So many ways to make an avocado drink. Leave off the sugar and go for a savory mood with herbs like fresh dill or tarragon. Use court bouillon (page 164) instead of milk for a vegan approach. Add a banana and flax meal. Try out a blend of avocado, pineapple, and lime juice. Get out the yogurt and the fresh spearmint. Or some cilantro and cucumber.

KBJ's Artichokes & JKJ's Tarragon Home Fries

You can fancy up artichokes until the old rockers come home, but nothing beats the classic way my mother, Kathleen Brown Johnson, served them. She and her generation must have sensed that a vegetable as grand as an artichoke should come to the table in all its glory. Mom even had a set of artichoke plates she bought when she lived in Carmel-by-the-Sea before the Second World War. You can see that the plates have an indentation for the melted butter as well as a place to stash your used leaves—real estate I've usurped in this photo for my home fries.

Recipe Note

Bring your artichokes to a low boil in a big pot with plenty of water so they can bob around elegantly while they cook. It takes awhile as you'd expect with big boys like most domestic artichokes are—like a good hour. When the chokes are done, a lower test leaf pulls off easily and a meaty morsel at the end of the leaf awaits. Serve with melted butter and dip the end of each leaf in the warm golden fat, using your teeth to pull the fleshy goodness away from the tougher inedible part. When you get to the center scoop out the whorl of fuzzy stuff and savor your very own artichoke bottom.

A medium to hot oven works for home fries. Cut your potatoes into stout wedges and toss them in oil, salt, paprika, and freshly minced tarragon right from the twig. Bake until soft inside, flipping and stirring once or twice so the edges of the wedges get all nice and crispy.

Summer Fare

In many ways the dynamics of summer mirror those of spring. We tend to think solstice late in June means tomatoes, peppers, squash, green beans, and sweet corn. Instead we find it takes awhile, including some scorching August dog days, for these prized numbers to do their thing. So in early summer, salads made from tender lettuces and zippy radishes must do. And they are a welcome relief from the flash cooked soups and warm salads that taste so great during the colder times of year.

Not to say this chapter is completely devoted to vegetables. It includes an inordinate number of sweet treats. From melons to brownies and around the back fence with the summer darlings, raspberries, ideas are here on how easy and affordable it is to pull homemade sweet nothings together. Admittedly there's more sugar and flour in Magical Brownies than we should probably eat, but what's to say. It's summertime. Still, for those looking for sweets without refined sugars and flours, check out the Laid Back Melon or the Gonzo Raspberry Shortcake. They're a groove.

Also, since once summer gets rolling, we want to be outside tilting our faces to the sun, there are plenty of quick fixes like bread salad and tostadas, both ultrafast and easy enough for cooks who are brand new to hippie kitchens and the idea of letting the measuring routine take a hike.

So it's all about getting on a roll with summer. Like the Moody Blues belted out in 1972:

"The sun is still shining, look at the view. The moon is still dining, with me and you.
Now that we're out here, open your heart. To the universe, of which we're a part."

Homemade Lemonade

Remember the days before canned pop when the man brought blocks of ice for the oak box in the kitchen? I don't but that doesn't stop me from imagining how we were before we started popping tabs and squabbling over the remote control. A glass of lemonade fresh squeezed by your mother or one of your aunts for Fourth of July was a real treat. Even the one you bought with fifteen cents from your kid brother stationed firmly behind his lemonade stand wasn't half bad. Homemade lemonade can still be a hit, especially when you skip the syrup heating routine and add red chile flakes.

Recipe Note

Squeeze the juice from fresh lemons, allowing about one for each glass of lemonade. It's nice to pick the seeds out rather than straining the juice so bits of pulp remain. Add water, sweeten with sugar, spike with red chile flakes, and pour over plenty of ice. Serve with swizzle sticks and watch how amazingly fast your cool drink of Homemade Lemonade disappears.

Details

Yes, most recipes say to make a syrup with the sugar first, but we never did. Half the fun was swirling your drink to keep the sugar in suspension. Plus that, when it's hot out, who feels like slaving over a stove? Yes, the syrup's nice and refined. But also yes, lemonade is way more likely to be happening thing if you get to side step the production.

Stoned Salad Rolls

Stoned. Stoner. The Stones. There was plenty of it going around in the Sixties—as far as I recall anyhow. Still, give a bunch of hippies four decades to get their act together, and they're ready to join the renaissance. Yes! We may have gone to extremes and lost our bearings for a bit, but our original ideas were on target. Now, before we split—before we take a flying leap off the planet and out into the great mystery—we're poised for an entirely subversive last hurrah. Dylan's still doing his thing, and on the British side of the pond Eric Clapton, the Rolling Stones, and the Moody Blues are rocking audiences around the world. So bring on the Stoned Salad Rolls. Bring on food free from the taint of factory farming and corporate processing. Fine with me to do the work of cooking the beans and smashing them up in my hippie kitchen. Ditto on washing the lettuce. It's honest labor. It's heavy, man. It's a stoner.

Recipe Note

Use your stout fork to smash up cooked lima beans (or whatever kind of bean you have cooked up) while they're heating in some oil. Season your refrieds with salt and cayenne pepper. Serve topped with blue cheese and wedges of lime. Alongside, offer a stack of spring lettuce leaves that stoners can use to roll their own.

Details

Washing and crisping the lettuce is the main job with this ultrafast offering, and it's nice to get the chore done in the cool of the morning when you've got a buzz going from your coffee.

Give your lovely leaves a dousing in a big bowl of water and drain. Then layer them in between some tea towels, roll the works up tidily, and stash in the fridge's crisper drawer. Or make like a salad spinner and put your leaves in a pillow case, step outside, and go for it.

On cheese, it's all about the blues for me. All kinds blue cheeses whether Gorgonzola, Roquefort, or Stilton—or one of the new American artisan varieties like those from Humbolt County or Oregon's Rogue River Valley. What flavor. The blues can really make the

Vanilla Fudge's

beat go on

and on

and on.

On Lettuce Leaves as Flat Bread—

The Vietnamese noodle shop around the corner got me into using lettuce leaves as flat bread. They serve big ruffled leaves along with basil and mint on the stem with their soups and eggy pancakes. Instead of filling up on bread, diners get their veggies. Also, serving whole leaves is easy on the cook and the eaters. Why we ever assumed lettuce always has to be chopped up into little salady pieces is puzzling. Unless, of course, way back when it got started, we only had eyes for haute French cuisine. Chuckle.

On Lima Beans & Garbanzos—

Lima beans are the best—especially home cooked. Almost as comforting as mashed potatoes. Not only are they easy, you get a whole pound of dry beans for the price of one of those little cans.

Just soak your limas—or any kind of bean you find interesting—over night. Rinse and bring them to a boil in fresh water before turning to a simmer. Some salt, onion, and minced garlic can go into the water to help the cause, although aren't at all required if you've no mood for the chopping board. A big pot of beans gives plenty to eat over four or five days plus a half dozen cartons to freeze away for later on down the pike.

Thawing a carton of beans makes whipping something up on the fly so easy an old stoner could pull it off. Warmed limas in olive oil and red wine vinegar with summer savory and toasted walnuts, for example, are great for late lunch with crackers or toast. Or try a similar treatment with garbanzos, roasted red peppers, Spanish olives, and toasted hazelnuts. With a jug of Dego red, you'll be cruising Led Zeppelin's "stairway to heaven."

What's Happening Bread Salad

The hipster crowd I ran with in Northern Arizona in the Sixties was way too busy hanging out in redrock canyons and climbing mountains to keep its finger on the pulse of the times. We really did get stuck in the Sixties.

Not to say that we didn't read and rack up our share of college degrees. But at least in my case, it was literature that attracted, not articles in Harpers *and the* New York Times *that would have kept me more informed.*

So I'd only vaguely heard of panzella, the bread salad from Italy, the first August not so long ago when I made the lunch we christened What's Happening Bread Salad. After I realized how delicious it is and went in search of formal recipes, I was gratified to find that between what the garden had to offer and my own intuition, I'd come up with what Italian peasants have been feasting on for centuries. It was as it should be since like a peasant, what little time I had for lunch I wanted to spend eating good food, not laboring over instructions and measuring things out.

Recipe Note

Cube day old bread. Toss with chopped tomatoes, garlic minced into salt, lots of fresh basil, and a crack of fresh black pepper. Dress with olive oil and red wine vinegar. That's it unless you want to pour a glass of red vino—and perhaps take a languid siesta after lunch.

Details

One of the secrets to this salad is the bread. You've got to use something with some tooth to it. I went for a sourdough whole wheat batard from a good bakery.

The other secret is vine-ripened tomatoes from your own garden or a farmers market. Interesting varieties of tomatoes that, like the Brandywine pictured, will bring genuine flavor to your feast.

As far as the basil goes, use a lot of it, not just a little leaf or two like some restaurants do to get by on the cheap.

To get the thin chiffonaded

On 100 Percent Whole Grain Breads—

I don't know why more bakers don't take some tips from *The Laurel's Kitchen Bread Book*. It offers a raft of recipes for completely whole grain breads that are entirely lovely. Laurel's "Loaf for Learning," in particular, turns out so light that people think it has white flour, when it's all in the kneading.

Ever since Laurel and company turned me on to the idea of getting whole grain nutrition with your food, I've left the world of refined grains and flours pretty much behind. Breads, cookies, pie crust, crepes. They all work great with whole grain flours.

So cop an attitude. Dump that white stuff. After all, wasn't it white flour that our Kindergarten teachers had us use for making paste when we were little kids?

basil that everyone loves, roll a stack of leaves into a fat cigar and start slicing. But if you've no patience for layering up your leaves, try a rustic chop of basil—or even whole leaves. For a weekday lunch, it's plenty good.

On Garlic Salt—

When I read somewhere about mincing garlic on a bed of salt to help break down the cloves, the light bulb went on. That bottled garlic salt complete with some unpronounceable things in it for freshness and free-running? No need for that faux, flavorless stuff anymore. Here was authentic garlic salt.

Recipes, Italians, & Imperial Measurements—

The British food writer Elizabeth David (1914-1992) gave much to the culinary map of today. She spoke seasonal in the 1940s and 1950s, way ahead of the curve. She spoke Mediterranean early on after extended stays in the sunny lands that hug that captivating deep blue sea.

David wasn't afraid to do things like plunge her hands into a bowl of salad greens to work the oil on properly. But this intrepid cook and author would only take so many leaps during her reign as a culinary goddess.

When it came to accepting the western world's penchant for using science as a lens through which cooking is understood, David saluted with all the vigor of a Brit with a stiff upper lip.

Here's what Artemis Cooper, her official biographer, writes of David's experience translating the art of Italian cooking into a structure and format English-speaking audiences expected:

"Generous and obliging as they were, Italian cooks took very little interest in quantities or measurements. Elizabeth had armed herself with a measuring jug, marked out in both imperial and metric measurements, and on occasions 'I stood over the cooks and simply forced them to show me what they meant by a handful.'"

Garlic Memories—

It was a spring day at Spaceway—Safeway if you must—back in the 1980s in Flagstaff, Arizona. There was this nice looking couple on the taller side, quiet as they waited in the checkout line, carrying themselves with a comportment that caught my eye. The fresh garlic and lemons they held in their hands looked like sedate jewels that only the privileged got to enjoy.

I felt chagrined over the garlic powder and plastic bottle of faux lemon juice back in my kitchen. Worse, I fretted that someone like me not only wouldn't take the time to use fresh ingredients, they probably wouldn't taste the difference if they did. I turned away from the well-heeled couple and tossed a couple candy bars in my basket.

Yet I wasn't a complete stranger to the world of real garlic and well remembered my mother making her own garlic oil for her Caesar salads. She had a bottle just the right size to contain some oil, and she'd put several cloves of peeled garlic in before letting it steep in the cool safety of the refrigerator.

So it was that somewhere along the line after my epiphany at Spaceway, I started buying fresh garlic to make garlic butter for sourdough bread. These days, I think nothing of mincing up a clove of garlic for soups and salads. There's almost always a bulb or two sitting out handy where I slice and dice. That plus some braids hanging about from the winter crop.

Gonzo Raspberry Shortcake

I'm not sure if former neighbor and friend, Marsha Buzan, is familiar with Hunter S. Thompson, but she does think this picture is the best. Certainly it's a new twist on red, white, and blue—something our totally irreverent gonzo journalist, the late Hunter S., would probably go for.

Recipe Note

Nestle a few room temperature raspberries onto a polenta waffle with a dab of cottage cream. Grate fresh nutmeg over the works.

Details

Polenta waffles are a lovely way to use leftover porridge. So consider the polenta left in the dinner pot the makings of breakfast. Just thin the cold porridge down with water, oil your waffle iron, and go to baking.

Cottage cream is merely cottage cheese turned smooth in your blender by using a tiny bit of water, lemon juice, milk, or what have you.

Bob's Polenta Waffles and Cottage Cream get fuller treatment
in the first volume of this measurefree cookbook trilogy: *Cooking Beyond Measure*.

Magical Brownies

*No, it's not what you're thinking, though it's not because I didn't consider putting Alice B. Toklas'
brownie-like hashish fudge in* Hippie Kitchen. *But here the magical ingredient is nothing more
than legal red wine. Cream cheese also makes an appearance. Cool, if it brings back memories of
Frank Zappa's Suzy Cream Cheese telling* the man *who wanted to ask her a few questions to
"Forget it!"*

Recipe Note

Cream a full size package of cream cheese, cube of butter, and a cup of raw sugar together with a few capfuls of pure vanilla extract or the scrapings of half a vanilla bean.

Add an egg and couple big spoons of pink hummus. From there enough cocoa from the bulk bins to make it chocolatey and a cup plus of whole wheat pastry flour with salt does the trick. Then some oat and wheat bran and a little kasha for crunch.

Bake in an oiled pan in a medium oven for twenty minutes or so. If, with the press of your finger your Magical Brownies seem too soft and in need of more time, turn the oven down and let the pan go a little longer—taking care to err on the moist, fudgy side. Cool some, but while still warm, pour red wine over the top. Frost with a concoction made from another package of cream cheese, more raw sugar, vanilla, and more cocoa powder.

Details

Brownies never did profess to be light creatures like cakes, and most brownie recipes call for no leavening. The result is the dense confection near and dear to American hearts. So not to worry here that whole wheat flour will be too heavy. It works great, and you get some nutrition with your decadence.

No biggie if you didn't score some kasha—cracked toasted buckwheat you can eat right from the sack—from bulk bins the last time you were shopping. Either make your brownies plain without crunch or go for walnuts or hazelnuts.

The secret with the frosting is to let the cream cheese come to room temp before stirring the sugar in. Then let the frosting set a while so the large raw sugar crystals melt—at least mostly. Once the sugar has had a chance to dissolve, whip in your cocoa powder which acts beautifully to thicken the brew into a fluffy frosting.

The pink hummus has you puzzled? Or turned off because you know that hummus is mainly beanpaste? Leave it out. I'm just always looking for ways to use more legumes, and this is sure a painless one.

On Pink Hummus—

Hummus made of smashed garbanzo beans and tahini (sesame seed butter) is traditional from the Middle East. But what happened in my hippie kitchen is that I only had pinto beans cooked up and also wanted a lean version of hummus.

What to do but toss the pintos the blender with enough water to rock & roll. Salt, vinegar, and I was there. Pink hummus for crackers, to thicken soups and sauces, as a dip for carrots and apples—and to add to brownie batter.

On Sweet Treats & Food Budgets—

We'd probably all be better off without sweet treats made from refined sugar, but if we must have them, here's the straight dope: go for homemade. Not only can you control what you put in your goodies, you can improve the bottom line on your food budget. That's because desserts whipped up at home are way less expensive than chocolate bars, packaged treats, and the designer ice creams so many are strung out on.

The late Elner Bartels—whose usual offhand line when I'd ask her some question or another was, "Gosh, kid, I don't know."—taught me about this kind of thrift. She went through the Great Depression and never forgot the power of a penny saved. Back when her parents slaved away at the broom factory in Oklahoma, Elner and her little brother had to wait in a cold house every day after school until their folks came home to light the fire in the woodstove.

Once Elner came of age and moved to Portland to raise her family, she found prosperity and with it could afford fixin's for sweets. Lemon meringue pie, cookies, banana bread, puddings. Those sorts of things were often on board at Elner's when you'd stop in. But they were always homemade—enabling Elner to save enough money over the years on a bank teller's salary to afford a comfortable life, including her own retirement condo for which she paid cash.

Whole Wheat Pasta Salad

I don't make much pasta because it's a processed product, expensive, and either from white flour or semolina, or in recent years whole grain versions akin to shoe leather. I did try my own homemade whole wheat noodles once that were delicious if not quite the project.

But whole grain pasta producers have been honing their skills, and I found some whole wheat fettucini that wasn't half bad. So during a spate of hot weather when I wanted something waiting for dinner, I put the pasta pot on in the cool of the morning.

But that's not entirely true. The other reason I got the pasta out was that I didn't have many vegetables on hand and needed to stretch them. Scarcity. It does have a way of nudging us outside our comfort zones.

Recipe Note

Toss cooked, drained whole wheat pasta with olive oil to keep the noodles from sticking as they cool. Add a mixed chop of flash cooked green tomato, zucchini, green beans, and sweet red pepper (page 45). Then minced garlic and parsley, coarse salt, and a grind of fresh black pepper.

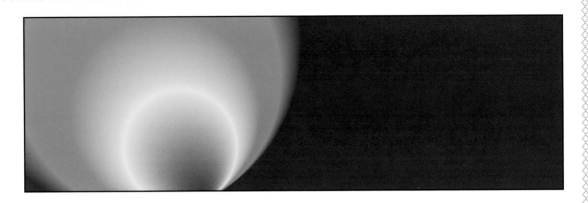

Details

Pasta goes in a big pot so it has lots of room to roil around in its bath of water. Do wait until the salted water has a good boil going to add the pasta, stirring at first to keep the noodles from sticking or the pot from boiling over—and bumping the heat down a few notches as needed. A small pour of oil into the water also helps the cause of keeping the pasta free to move around in the kettle without clinging to its brothers and sisters. It's done when it's tender. To figure that out you can either do the sensible thing and chomp on a strand or go for the flamboyant trick of flinging a piece on the wall, where the developed starch makes it sticks if it's done.

The vegetables are a function of what's in season. This is an adaptable salad that could roll with whatever's in your garden, comes in your Consumer Supported Agriculture (CSA) box, or is purchased from your farmers market or responsible natural food grocer.

On Scarcity—

It's always a surprise how my cooking and eating patterns change when I allow the larder to get depleted. Prize foods from the land of milk and honey go first. Cheesy quesadillas, berries and cream—all the meow-meow things. Beyond that, even not having a zillion vegetables around can be enlightening and result in things like this pasta salad.

Scarcity has also schooled me in early spring before the lettuces are edible. When I go out to get something green from the garden, what do I find but parsley, sage, rosemary, and thyme—all of them strutting their heady stuff. Uncertain but willing to be a trooper, I forage ahead cutting bunches, picking sprigs, and plucking leaves.

Soon I have a beautiful minced blend on the chopping board, fragrant with the time of ages and entirely delicious whether tossed with new potatoes, whole grains, pasta, or baked spaghetti squash.

> Are you going to Scarborough Fair?
> Parsley, sage, rosemary, and thyme...
>
> Simon and Garfunkel, 1966.

On Scarcity When the Wall Came Down—

Cynthia Harriman directs the Food and Nutrition Strategies for Oldways Preservation Trust—the Boston group that opposes what founder K. Dun Gifford calls techno-food.

When Harriman was in the Czech Republic in 1990 just after the Iron Curtain fell, people were beside themselves over juicy, red melons.

"Watermelon season started and that was the only fruit you could get anywhere. But rather than complain about the lack of variety, the Czechs were excited," she said. "There they were with all this pent-up emotion. They really appreciated the melons having their moment in the sun."

Scarcity. It's true that it makes things precious—and gives rise to much appreciation. There's no room for the tired and unappreciative "tomatoes coming out my ears" refrain here. Instead, the idea is that there won't be any more of these fleeting fresh babies for another whole year, so we better cherish them while we can.

On Consumer Supported Agriculture—

A good way to get started eating seasonally is by joining a Consumer Supported Agriculture (CSA) group in your area. For an annual fee, you get a box of produce weekly during the growing season from a local farmer. You also help strengthen your own community by keeping your food dollars close to home.

Plus, because you never know what will be in your box, you learn to go with the flow and experiment with a full range of vegetables, fruits, and herbs that might have otherwise remained strangers.

Warm Taco Salad with Crook Neck Squash

Sometimes in early summer it's cool enough to want a warm salad. This one has lots of peppers that, like the album, are "guaranteed to raise a smile." So space out with the Beatles' St. Pepper's Lonely Hearts Club Band and head off to the kitchen for this ultrafast taco salad.

Recipe Note

Flash cook onions, peppers, crook neck squash, and garlic in a heavy pan on high heat with enough water to keep things moist (page 45). Fold in some lima beans. Season with salt and top with fresh cilantro, Monterrey Jack cheese, and cayenne. Warm a corn tortilla or five to go with.

Details

If you're wondering why I didn't use pintos or black beans here, it's because I had limas cooked up. Black beans, especially, might have made for some good visuals in this dish, but so it goes when you're keeping things simple and working with what you have on hand.

Your choice on the peppers. I like some kick so I used Anaheims and a jalapeño.

Turned On Eggplant Pizza

The leftover eggplant you use for this pizza has way more flavor than when it's hot off the grill the night before.

Recipe Note

Slice eggplants in half and oil the cut surface lightly. Grill over the low heat that's left once dinner's done and the coals are dying down. The next day, top these luscious leftovers with a chop of lettuce and basil dressed with olive oil and red wine vinegar. Feta and paprika over the top makes things yummy and pretty, and salt and fresh black pepper finish this pizza ever so nicely. Serve with a fork or go outside and enjoy like street food.

Details

One slice through center and a light brush of oil is all it takes to ready medium sized eggplants for the grill. Eggplant flesh is a magnet for oil, so a light swipe with your hand or a pastry brush is a good approach. Over low heat with the barbeque lid on, eggplants soften and mellow into delectable fare.

When you're building your pizzas, work the oil over the chopped basil and lettuce before putting it on the eggplants. The oil helps keep the basil from discoloring. Also once you get greens coated, the vinegar beads up beautifully offering tiny tart hits of flavor.

Laid Back Melon

Food's got to be laid back in the summertime. In the case of Laid Back Melon, there's not even a dish to wash.

Recipe Note

Fill the cavity of your cantaloupe with cottage cream (page 82), lavender hummus, or yogurt. Sprinkle on wheat germ, flax meal, or oat bran. Top with red chile flakes, zest, and lime juice for flavor that leaps right out of the rind.

❋ On Lavender Hummus—

Cooked red kidney beans turn lavender when you whiz them up into a hummus. Just like pink hummus in Magical Brownies (page 84), if given half a chance, lavender hummus can become a basic, highly adaptable foodstuff in your hippie kitchen. And, adding lavender makes it even more exciting. You can use fresh or dried lavender leaves. You can use the flowers for a lemony, citrus tang or the leaves for a nose reminiscent of rosemary. Whatever approach you take, go lightly and taste your way into this flowery herbal world. You can also augment your lavender hummus any way you like, adding things like almond butter, dried figs, honey, and lemon juice. Then again, you can leave your blend fairly plain to serve as a bass note for things like Laid Back Melon. As with Magical Brownies, if you can't get behind this pretty pastel hummus, don't get up tight. Feel free to stuff your cantaloupe with whatever you like, even classic vanilla ice cream from responsible dairies and producers.

Arfie Luf Tostadas

The first time I had a tostada was in Phoenix, Arizona, at Alberta Larsen Jones' house. Our family had just moved to the desert, and us kids weren't too sure about the Mexican food everyone seemed to love. But Mom wanted to visit Alberta—one of the Arfies, five high school chums from Onawa, Iowa, where she grew up. And Alberta wanted to welcome us with tostadas and Arfie Luf.

Crispy circular corn tortillas you could pick up. Each bite an enticing cheesy, beany morsel, with just enough lettuce and onion to be interesting. I was sold and even tried a little of the hot sauce Alberta offered. Now, back home in Portland, Oregon, when I make tostadas, I still think of Alberta and how the Arfies always signed their notes to each other "Arfie Luf."

Recipe Note

Warm corn tortillas on a griddle in oil. Spread warmed refried beans on your tortillas and top with grated longhorn cheese, green onions, and thinly sliced lettuce. Offer salsa or hot sauce for those who love their spice and Kristy's Guacamole (page 60) for creamy dreamy fans.

Details

Refried pinto beans are traditional in Mexican food, although cooks in hippie kitchens know how fun it is to experiment with refrieds from limas, black beans, red beans, and even garbanzos. It's all good.

Iceberg lettuce was the only game in town back in 1960 when I bit into my first tostada. It's still the only thing happening in many Mexican restaurants because it's crunchy and an excellent keeper. But like so many of us, I love all the beautiful green leaf lettuces we're getting these days. Especially when you get your hands on freshly picked garden lettuce, you'll discover a subtle, lovely flavor that lifts summertime into a new dimension.

On Filled Things—

Something wonderful happens to food when it's gathered together in nice tidy bundles. Mexican tacos and tostadas, French crepes, Vietnamese salad rolls, Chinese eggrolls, Russian blintzes—and even American sandwiches. All of a sudden food—especially veggies—is fun. In an instant, potentially boring fare like refried beans, lettuce, and cheese become very user-friendly and thus get friendly smiles from users.

On Corn Tortillas & Whole Grain Nutrition—

For years I happily ate corn tortillas thinking they had whole grain nourishment. Alas, I recently discovered that most tortillas are made from husked, degerminated corn. But sometimes one door has to close before another can open.

Out I went searching and what did I find but some excellent corn tortillas made from whole, sprouted corn. No surprise that they come from a California company, Food for Life, the same producer that makes the line of sprouted, whole grain Ezekiel breads.

On Tostadas & Cheese Crisps—

Tostadas, yes, when there are *frijoles* around. Often, though, it's cheese crisps and salsa that's the mainstay. Let's face it; we're spoiled and think we're out of groceries if all we have is beans.

You could call them quesadillas, but back in the Sixties when we were exploring just how far out on the edge we could get and still keep on truckin', we just called 'em cheese crisps.

They were hits around our woodstoves with a snowstorm howling outside, and they were hits off our camp stoves whether in the bottom of the Grand Canyon, up on the San Francisco Peaks, or by the banks of the Middle Fork of the Salmon where we watched our rafts bob in the evening light on luminescent rippling water.

Cheese crisps are no brainers, which is one reason they worked so well for us in the Sixties. They're good as well, which is why we still make them after all these crazy years.

Arfie Luf—

Christy Moore, aged 91, is the only Arfie left. When I called to tell her about naming a recipe in memory of the Arfies, she got to talking.

"Your mother's folks had a cabin out at Blue Lake, and they always had us girls out. We swam and boated, and we sang too since Dot, one of the Arfie's, played the ukulele. Then in the winter Alberta's father harnessed up his big bob sled and took us for rides. We made our own fun, you know—and we were never bored."

How many times have we heard our elders tell us this—not only about homespun fun, but homemade

On Fresh Salsa—

Fresh salsa comes together in late summer like a grand psychedelic flashback. Chop peppers, onions, garlic, and tomatoes as politely as your patience permits. Lots of fresh lime juice and you're good to go, although cilantro can help the cause as well. For this salsa I used jalapeños for the heat and some lime green gypsy peppers because they were around.

Salsa making really isn't my favorite because of the fussy dicing routine. Still, in twenty minutes I had a big bowlful—and the clean up wasn't bad. It lasted three or four days during which we dosed most everything we ate with it.

On Fresh Hot Chile Peppers—

If any food can teach us about fresh flavor, hot chiles can. Close your eyes the next time you encounter salsa fresca and see if you can't detect the great flavor that fresh green chile carries. Yes, it has heat, but so much more: the sun and the fields and cool clear water are all bound up in these shiny verdant pods.

It's true that some chiles are red or orange when they're fresh. Mostly, though, we think of red chiles as dried creatures. An Anaheim, for example, is usually green when it comes from the vine and red once it dries. (Picture the ristras—strings of red chile—common in the Southwest.) To me dried chiles are akin to raisins, nice enough in their own way, but definitely lacking the lush flavor of their fresh counterparts.

Roasted Sweet Corn & Giant Corn Necklaces

It was an experience living in the Hopi village of Sipaulovi in the 1980s. During the week I taught school, but at night and on weekends I cooked with the ladies and got included in things like the sweet corn harvest. I remember it well. We drove out to Alph and Alfreda Secakuku's (see-KA-koo-koo) field at dawn.

The corn had roasted all night long covered over with corn leaves. Alph and the other men opened up the deep pit and the smell of fresh baked roasting ears mingled with the arid morning. There we stood with the first of the corn in our hands, peeling back the husks and biting into the sweet milky flesh. "It's kwangwa," Alfreda said, pronouncing it good in Hopi.

We loaded up the corn and took it to Alfreda's mother's house—in the Hopi way, the men grow the corn, but once it's harvested it becomes the property of

the women who manage the supply. At the house, the sweet corn was the centerpiece of a breakfast feast: eggs, freshly baked round Hopi bread, pinto beans, and roasted green chiles. Afterward we husked and strung necklace upon giant necklace that joined the ristras of chiles under the eaves to dry.

Recipe Note

I don't have a pit in my backyard or big fields of corn like the Secakuku's do. Still, putting trays of wetted roasting ears in a slow oven works after a fashion, even though a big roaster pan with a lid would more accurately mimic the steaming that takes place when corn is pit roasted. As we ate we even tried to be thankful for Mother Corn the way the Hopi have been for centuries.

This is a great way to put up corn for winter since drying needs only the power of the sun. The giant necklaces dried great even up here in the Pacific Northwest. Corn preserved this way really does feed your soul in the middle of winter after it's dropped into a pot of boiling water to revive.

Latina Peaches

For these peaches, pass on the ginger and step away from the bourbon. Instead grab some limes, red chile, and salt. Yep. Latina Peaches take a deep curtsey south of the border. Here's to you and su familia, Argelis.

Recipe Note

Slice up ripe peaches and toss with red chile flakes, sugar, salt, a tad of finely minced garlic, and fresh lime juice plus a little zest from the rind if you're not feeling too languid.

Details

When we were messing around with jicama in one of my cooking classes at Portland's Whole Foods in The Pearl, aficionado Naomi Pollock talked about how they'd fixed it in Mexico: tossed with lime and chile. Then I ran across something in *Gourmet* magazine called chile salt: a garlic clove pounded with forty of those little dried *chiles de árbol* and a good half cup of salt. They even get fancy and char the chiles and garlic on the grill first. *Gourmet* uses the salt with sticks of jicama and mango and watermelon, something that sounds hunky dory to me, if not as easy-breezy as my approach with Latina Peaches.

On Hot Chile Peppers—

A general rule of thumb with chiles is: the smaller the hotter. Things like Thai chiles and cayenne peppers come to mind. Also jalapeños and serranos. Then there are the Big Jim Anaheims, great for rellenos and for first roasting and then freezing up in small batches for winter to fry with potatoes or whatever grabs you. (See page 62.) They have some heat, but nothing like the biting little terrier versions of hot chile peppers.

Chiles de árbol that *Gourmet* recommends are small, but much tamer than fiery Thai and cayenne peppers. And *chiles de árbol* are the type of pepper that is usually crushed and sold as red chile flakes or *quebrado* (broken in Spanish). Certainly this isn't exclusively the case, as companies all over the world make red chile flakes from various species of capsicum. Still when I did a taste test with Latina Peaches, I found the heat from home ground *chiles de árbol* comparable to that of generic red chile flakes.

On Putting Peaches Up for the Freezer—

It's easy to sock away some peaches for winter. Just pit your fruit and roast it lightly in a medium oven. It's a way to mimic the heat of parboiling without actually dunking food in water where nutrients leach from the cut surfaces. You can either freeze the peaches on baking trays before bagging or simply lay your bags into the freezer flat so the fruit doesn't turn into an iceberg. Once the dark days descend, it's time to enjoy your peaches on cereal and in cobblers and pies. Or if you want to try them in a warm salad of Bourbon Chard Ribbons, check out page 134.

On Chutneys, Peach & Otherwise—

My mother loved chutney, but only Major Grey's. With all due respect to the British Empire and your spirit, Mom, not all variations on the classic theme are foolishness. It is possible to simmer down an entirely mouth watering chutney from fruit like peaches as long as they're laced with enough diced onions, minced serranos, raisins, and a beguiling combo of spices and vinegar.

With peaches I'm thinking brown mustard seeds popped in hot oil under a lid and then enough cinnamon, nutmeg, and cloves to make a roux that would knock a Frenchy's socks off. A great paste to blend into your cooked fruit, peppers, and onions—whether you incorporate some of the more traditional turmeric, coriander, and cumin or not—the latter of which could be nicely used whole as seeds and added to the hot oil with the mustard seeds.

Frozen Summer Fruits in Shades of Red, Green, & Blue

Eating frozen cherries and grapes is like having first rate sorbet without the sugar. Blueberries freeze beautifully as well and are great on cereal or with milk & sugarama, not to mention in pancakes. So get a life in shades of red, green, and blue. Fruit is at its best price during harvest —and freezing is light years easier than canning.

Recipe Note

Cherries and grapes freeze beautifully. You don't even need to take them off the stems. Just freeze your clean fruit in large bags. To enjoy cherries and grapes, put a few of these innocent sugar free delights in a bowl on the table after dinner. Since they thaw right away and are best on the frozeny side, wait until you're ready for dessert to get them out.

Blueberries are another summer fruit that are superb frozen. Put a handful or two into a bowl of milk and sprinkle on some brown sugar. That molasses hit from brown sugar is especially great, whether or not you add cinnamon.

Details

Lay your bags flat when you first stash them in the freezer. That way the fruit won't clump, and you can get however much you want out at the time.

Pacific Rim Seafoam Pie

I figured someone would get twitted out if the mint, tarragon, and cucumbers went missing in pages touting Summer Fare. So here they are blended into a pie that could have come from Japan as easily as it did this side of the Pacific Rim. No seeding the cukes. No peeling. Just blending them and the spearmint with lime juice, sugar, tofu, and melted agar agar flakes, straight from ocean's kelp beds.

This pie even features a crumb shell with oil instead of butter to keep this cool refreshing offering well within the impeccable land vegans inhabit. Between the whole grains, tofu, and green herbs, you could call this a complete meal. I imagine it would even work without the sugar as savory fare.

Recipe Note

Mix a blend of wheat germ, oat bran, and flax meal—about a cup and a half total—together with a couple pinches of salt and enough sugar to sweeten things. Stir in oil until you have a mixture that will press into a large pie plate. Smooth the edges of the rim down nicely so the pointy bits don't burn and try to get an even thickness across the bottom. Bake until browned in a medium oven, watching it like a hawk since it doesn't take long. Cool on a rack to keep your crust crisp.

For the filling, whiz up a cucumber, fresh lime juice, tub of tofu, sugar, pinch of salt, fresh spearmint, and fresh tarragon in the blender. Simmer two big spoons of agar agar powder in a little water on the stove until it's dissolved, adding more water as you go to keep it from solidifying (page 114). Add the agar agar brew to the filling and blend before pouring the works into the cooled shell. The pie will set up in the refrigerator and be cool enough to slice in a couple hours. It's best enjoyed the same day while the bottom crust is still crisp—although some like the syrupy action that develops by day two.

Details

If you've not made a crumb crust before, know that you've got to watch it like a teenage son. So err on the low side with the heat, peek frequently, turn the pan around often, and pull it out early than later since the crust will continue cooking in the lingering heat of the pie plate.

The filling is pretty easy as the cucumber, minus the bitter ends, goes in the blender with the tofu, sugar, and salt. The cuke peeling along with the herbs gives the filling its seafoam color.

I used several handfuls of spearmint and tarragon leaves, which would probably be too much for non-vegans who might not be hip to having a mini herb salad whizzed into their pie. Then again, it's mostly vegans we're thinking of here, given that tofu's our base for the filling.

Spearmint is always my choice of mints, so much so that I don't even grow peppermint.

On Agar Agar—

Agar agar is a gelling substance that comes from kelp. It's available in flakes at natural foods markets, but this time I found some powder at the Asian store. When I first walked in and asked for agar agar, the husband owner couldn't understand me and said, "Salad rolls right here." Trying not to get a big head about being so beyond mere salad rolls, I eventually found the agar agar flakes. When I went to pay, the wife of the team realized what I was about and showed me the powdered form. "It's easier," she said. So that's what I used. The little packet of powder had two big spoons in it, just the right amount for most desserts including this pie. It was a couple dollars just like the larger package of flakes, but it was worth it to talk cooking with a woman from across the Pacific Rim. Besides she was right. The powder was easy.

On Muddling—

Whizzed up herbs in a pie might strike those who take their muddling seriously as unrefined. But think about tabbouleh, the grain salad with chopped mint and parsley that Middle Easterners love. Or the mint that goes into a cucumber-mint raita, the cool yogurt dish from India.

If you must muddle your mint and tarragon for this pie, however, put some leaves in a mortar with part of your sugar. Use a pestle to press and bruise the greens, before adding enough water to carry the oils you've released through a strainer and into the filling.

Fall Bounty

Fall. Autumn. Indian Summer. By any name, it's the season when harvest makes us feel as wealthy and royal as Celeste and HH (page 36). But like the froggy couple that has jumped from their ponds and gotten lovey-dovey in this measurefree cookbook trilogy, the richness we experience is down to earth, steeped in brandy and bourbon, made mysteriously witchy and herbaceous by Mother Nature herself.

Fall really does have to be about the best. Fluttering golden aspens. Roads lined with wild Black-Eyed Susans. Lugs of apples. Truckloads of corn. Fat fresh figs, with their teeny tiny figgy seeds.

The first frost comes and summer's crazy party is over. Yet, another happening scene opens in the earth's annual rounds. Suddenly we could care less about melon. We want squash. We want dark leafy greens, roasted plums, and pie crust made from things like flax meal and oat bran. We want to toast nuts and grow sprouts in a jar by the kitchen sink. It's as if a spell has been cast. Yet, it's as it should be. Mr. Mellow Yellow, Quite Rightly Donovan Leitch knew that. Yes. Donovan and his Season of the Witch. Remember?

When I look out my window,
Many sights to see.
And when I look in my window,
So many different people to be
That it's strange, so strange.
You've got to pick up every stitch,
You've got to pick up every stitch,
Mm, must be the season of the witch,
Must be the season of the witch, yeah,
Must be the season of the witch.

Fall Bounty

Cinnamon Brandy Apples

That plaintive voice of Neil Young: "I wanna live with a cinnamon girl." Ah, yes, if you make these homey stovetop apples, you just might have to go put on the tune. Even if the album's not around, once you're so beautifully fed, you are on your way to being "a dreamer of pictures...chasing the moonlight."

Recipe Note

Dissolve a spoon of arrowroot powder or cornstarch in a little cold water before adding to grated apple laced with lemon juice for a simmer. Cinnamon, nutmeg, pure vanilla extract, and little brandy turns these apples goopy and homey and good. Spoon Cinnamon Brandy Apples over most anything: oatmeal with raisins, steamed amaranth, nutty quinoa, cottage cream, plain yogurt. Or skip the stovetop scene and bake your apples under a lattice of Flax Meal Pie Crust (page 124).

Details

Thickening agents like arrowroot and cornstarch clump in hot water, so make sure you've drawn from the cold tap. Use a teaspoon to a third cup of liquid. A heavy bottom pan plus vigilant stirring over fairly high heat will get the thickening action happening in short order.

I usually put the spices in while the fruit is softening and save the vanilla for the end. Then all's left to do is close your eyes, dream of pictures, and inhale the sweet down home aroma. How much cinnamon and nutmeg? Cinnamon's forgiving and adds sweetness, so a small spoonful works. On nutmeg, it doesn't take much of this peppery spice, so go for a conservative pinch until you find your stride. If vanilla sounds strange added to cooked apples, here's my story: It was Williams, Arizona. The Sixties. Bobbie Smith's kitchen. She was making applesauce and used a generous pour of vanilla. I've not tasted better before or since. Here's to you, Bobbie. You and Smitty and Wesley were such a righteous trip.

You'll notice there's lemon, not sugar or honey in Cinnamon Brandy Apples. That's because most of our apples have been bred to accommodate Americans' notorious lust for sweetness. It's also because once we quit dosing fruits automatically with extra sugars, we get a chance to truly savor the flavor—flavor that is often surprisingly plenty sweet in its own right.

Ditto on butter. There's none called for here. But I confess that a little pat allowed to melt over the top of warm apples can make you feel like chasing some serious moonlight.

On Apple Varieties—

During the fall it's a trip to get half a dozen different apples and line them up for a taste test. From there it's also fun to see how each behaves when cooked either stovetop or in the oven—what it carries in the way of flavor after heat turns it soft—how the form of the apple holds up and whether it tends to turn to sauce.

I often have Galas or the somewhat sweeter Fujis on hand since slices straight off the core are so crisp and bright—albeit in the category of soda pop apples bred for the infamous American sweet tooth. Then again a tree I espaliered along the driveway gives equally sweet Jonagolds that invariably get munched directly from the branches. Still, when I get on a jag of eating Smoked Edam or Gouda and dark rye breads, I like tart Granny Smith's or Pippins—apples that invariably lead to a pie.

The main thing is that we've come a long way from the desert of Delicious apples that dominated after the Second World War when we homogenized everything in sight.

On Honey & Sugar—

Friend Laurie Mercier said that when she was in Japan she had to seek out sweets when she wanted them. "They just aren't part of the Japanese diet," she said. "And you know, I didn't see a heavy person the whole time I was there."

Even if you're not in Taj Mahal's heavy hippie mama camp, health care professionals question diets dosed in sugars for a range of reasons. And, of course, culinary observers around the globe point out that Americans are known for their excessive consumption of the coy and cloying white crystal. What to say except to go easy on the sugarama and the honey, whether it's Van Morrison's Tupelo or clover from bees that are tended by keepers with good ethics.

On Fresh Figs—

It goes without saying that if you've got some fresh figs they'd work great here simmered with spices and nestled in under the lattice crust.

For the Intrepid—

Try Cinnamon Brandy Apples and oat bran sprinkled on warm garbanzos spiked with some seeded and minced jalapeño, juice from a whole fresh lemon or lime, and a pinch of salt. Raisins and walnuts finish this wowie zowie, bountiful breakfast.

Beans in your morning cereal sound bizarre? Hey, this is rustic, affordable food—and way more delicious than it sounds with a hip Thai-style blend of sour, spice, sweet, and salt.

But, if you simply must have yogurt or milk on your cereal alone, Frank Zappa sure isn't going to give a flying wowie zowie rip.

Flax Meal Pie Crust

No wheat or other kinds of flour in your food plan? Flax meal and oat bran can help you work it out. As Lennon & McCartney wrote in 1965, "Life is very short, and there's no time for fussing and fighting, my friend."

Recipe Note

Work bits of room temperature caramelized goat cheese into flax meal, oat bran, and salt. Add a little balsamic vinegar and enough water to bring the dough together. Roll out and cut into strips for a lattice. Weave over the top of Cinnamon Brandy Apples (page 120) or Roasted Plums (page 128) and bake this rustic top crust until it's nut brown. If you want shine—something I didn't bother with in the one pictured here—brush the crust with milk or an egg white plus a little water beaten with a fork.

On Crusts: Top, Bottom, & Crumb—

There's no way around it, pie crust is high test food—a delicious mix of carbs and fat. For years, I shunned crusts completely, thinking them too rich. But as the Greeks knew, the middle ground is so much more stable than extremes.

If you're thinking that middle ground when it comes to pie crust means skipping the bottom layer and zeroing in on a golden topper, right on. So go ahead, have your pie crust and eat it too.

Because it's made with cheese and not butter or oil, count on this crust for some protein as well as a consistency somewhere between crumb and flake. Really quite lovely, this arena of using cheese in place of pure fat for pie crust. Next time I'm thinking cheddar. It would match the slices of cheddar men, particularly, so often like on top of their apple pie.

Details

I like to work flax meal into lots of things because it's nutty and heart-healthy too—so the latest word is anyhow.

The best pie crusts I've ever had use a third to a half cup of fat for every cup of dry ingredients. For this crust I opted for gjetost (YET-oast), caramelized goat cheese from Norway, although any number of cheeses would work from soft Camembert and Brie to salty Gorgonzola and good old cheddar.

On the liquid, the idea is to get by with as little as possible, using just enough to bind the dough into a ball without kneading in toughness. Start with a few good shakes of balsamic vinegar which appeals so in autumn, pressing the dough together gently. Keep this technique going with sprinklings of ice water until you have a ball of dough you can roll out.

No patience for all that fussy dough ball and rolling stuff? Make a crumb crust topping instead. It's basically the same trip except you stir in just enough liquid to get some nice crumbles. You can even mix in some scissored Medjool dates and a chop of walnuts.

On Gluten—

Gluten comes from wheat and barley and rye, but not corn or rice.

Oats are free of gluten as well, although if they're milled at the same facilities as the grains containing gluten, cross-contamination can occur.

Roasted Plums

These babies slow roasted in the oven come autumn are such "lovin' spoonfuls" that they will definitely have you believing in magic. Even fruit that isn't quite ripe turns soft and flavorful whether you savor it plain or nestled down under a gluten-free crust (page 112).

Recipe Note

Halve plums, popping the pits out with a paring knife. Put in a ceramic baking dish and roast in a low oven for a half hour or more.

Preserving Stoned Fruits—

Clearly peaches could stand in for plums here. And both roasted fruits freeze nicely in their saucy elegance, should you have enough to put by for winter. If you do, come the dark days, these preserved stoned fruits will have much to say about your home and hearth. (See page 108.)

Rocker Note—

John Sebastian wrote "Do You Believe in Magic" in 1965 and the song served as the title of the Lovin' Spoonful's popular album. More, Sebastian and the band had electrified their sound well ahead of the curve—so much so that after hearing the band do a concert, future psychedelic rockers who became the Grateful Dead, hung up their acoustic axes.

Blue Corn Waffles

These waffles aren't traditional with the Hopi even though the tribe is known for its blue corn cuisine. I made them after hipster and gardener from Northern Arizona, Bob Goforth, sent up a lid of blue corn flour plus a handful of seeds to keep the circle turning. Thanks, Bob. What a cool way to "feed your head." ~White Rabbit, Surealistic Pillow, Grace Slick, 1967.

Recipe Note

Whisk an egg, milk, shot of oil, and polite slug of vinegar together.

Stir in blue corn flour leavened with soda and seasoned with salt and red chile flakes.

Bake in an oiled waffle iron.

Details

Vinegar fizzes with the soda to lighten these waffles, and the red chile gives them serious la-la. Make your batter thick enough to spoon into the waffle iron since it's mainly batters that are too thin that tend to stick.

If you aren't into making waffles, do feel free to turn these into pancakes or cornbread. They're all family. Or you can do like Bob did and make blue corn flour crepes. I tried these too, and they smelled like the Southwest after a thunderstorm.

On Avoiding Sticky Wicket Waffles—

I've dug my share of failed waffles out of the little square indentations. That was back when I didn't oil the iron nicely with a pastry brush, and

On Blue Corn—

I still remember the time after I'd moved from Hopiland home to Flagstaff. It was back in our rafting days and someone wanted to take some blue corn meal along on a trip down the Colorado through the Grand Canyon. So I called Alfreda out on Second Mesa.

"How can we get some blue corn for the river trip?" I asked.

Her answer? "Grow it."

Tough love from a Hopi woman for sure.

I arched my middle class brow and thought, "Forget it."

The times, though, they really did change. This season I'll be sowing the blue corn kernels Bob sent along with slew of other things. Perhaps not the big time thrills of a romp through the Grand but an experience sure to bring its own enduring joy.

more critically, when I used too much liquid in the batter. It's true that sometimes I can get by with a thin batter that results in the cracker-like, crispy waffles, but the safest bet until you get your sea legs is to go with a thicker than thinner batter, something akin to thinned mashed potatoes. At one point in my waffle making, I thought milk products made things stick, but I never got very scientific about it and can't really say it wasn't because those batters were simply too thin.

The main thing is that making waffles isn't as much of trip as I used to think. Plus, they're better than pancakes because there's no possibility of doughy middles. Sort of like the difference between baking a cake in a regular pan and a Bundt pan—the indentation in the center helps the cake cook through.

Finally, on the horror of lifting the lid and finding your lovely waffle pulled apart and clinging to the top and the bottom. Never fear. All it takes—given that your batter was thick enough—is closing the iron and letting the heat finish doing its thing. In another minute or two, the miraculous will have happened. The waffle will be waiting under the lid in one dazzlingly fabulous piece.

On a Roll with Blue & Yellow Corn—

It goes without saying that you can substitute yellow for blue cornmeal and still rock. You can also easily turn waffle batter into pancakes or cornbread. The gist here is to make pancake batters thinner that waffle batters so they pour onto a griddle easily and aren't too thick to cook through. On the cornbread route, follow the lead of your waffle batter, augmenting it with whole wheat pastry flour, a little honey, and another egg or two. That way you'll get a moist cornbread plus leftovers to toast into croutons and toss into to Bourbon Chard Ribbons (page 134).

Most recipes that use cornmeal—whether for waffles, pancakes, or bread—call for at least part wheat flour and sometimes I go that route. Mainly, though, I like to explore what happens with 100 percent cornmeal and have found I can control how well what I'm making holds together with the amount of oil and eggs I use.

On Leavening—

I remember a novel set in the early 1800s in which the older women criticized the young marrieds for using the new quick leavenings. It was just one line, but it's stayed with me. The idea of how little the old guard thought of the young moderns and their penchant for being in such a hurry they couldn't wait for yeast to work. There's not a reason other than time that you couldn't use yeast to make Blue Corn Waffles, using a ratio of a teaspoon of yeast softened in warm water for every cup of dry ingredients. But what can we say; we get more biz-biz all the time it seems and want things on the double.

Sodas can leave an off taste in quick breads if you goof and use too much, which is one reason so many recipes call for baking powder. But as my all time favorite cookbook, *Laurel's Kitchen,* points out, you can make your own aluminum-free baking power using one part soda to two parts cream of tartar. Frankly, whenever I have some of this made up I use it instead of straight soda. But I can be a very lazy hippie cook. Besides, isn't it the Irish that use nothing but soda in their famous bread?

Bourbon Chard Ribbons

I usually go for kale, not Swiss chard. But turning chard into fettuccini like ribbons makes this warm salad in the Southern tradition just peachy. You could even add cornbread croutons to really capture an "I've got one more silver dollar," Allman Brothers experience.

Recipe Note

Toast cumin seeds in plenty of good oil and stir in a pinch of cayenne and minced garlic. Add chard that you've sliced into ribbony threads. Splash with bourbon during the minute or two it takes to flash cook the greens on full blast heat (page 45). When you dish up, garnish chard ribbons with wheat berry sprouts, home preserved peaches, a squeeze of lemon, toasted pecan halves, and cornbread croutons (page 132).

Details

Making chard ribbons isn't hard since they don't need to be perfect. Simply gather a nice bunch of leaves with the thicker parts of the stems removed (page 141) into a tidy bundle. Then roll it up tightly and slice it off.

Use a small palmful of cumin seeds to lots of oil and stir until fragrant like cooks from India do. I pull my cast iron wok off my electric burner momentarily when I add the garlic so it doesn't burn. (Yes. I'm still cooking on my aunt's old stove. It hasn't broken yet, so we thrifty Scandahoovians are carrying on.) Do keep stirring at this stage, but avoid taking a deep breath as volatiles released by these high-powered aromatics can be quite the lungful.

Peaches in the fall can come right from your canning jars or your freezer (pages 108 & 128). Beautiful yellow-gold hemispheres that you put away during the peak of harvest. I love to can peaches but usually can't spare the time. Pitting a dozen fruits, though, and roasting the halves in the oven briefly before bagging them for the freezer is an exceedingly quick, easy fix.

If peach skins are too tough for you, they'll slip off pretty much once the peaches are roasted. Seems a waste of delicious fiber to me, but whatever turns you on.

On Toasting Nuts & Seeds—

Like any nutmeat, pecans can be toasted either stovetop over medium heat or in a 300 degree oven. The key here is not to turn the heat up so the nuts keep their nutrients and don't burn. Admittedly pecans are pricey and best reserved for special. That's why it's nice to use them in large pieces so they'll get plenty of attention. For everyday, though, peanuts are darn good food and have the added attraction of being pre-roasted in the bulk bins. Then again you can't go wrong with walnuts or hazelnuts.

There's also pumpkin seeds, called pepitas when they're toasted. It's fun to do a batch of pepitas in the fall. They pop and puff up when roasted in either a dry or an oiled skillet. Salted they are the bees knees—as are toasted sesame seeds either left whole or crushed still warm from the pan in your mortar and pestle.

On Sprouts & Thrift—

I know the value of sprouted food from firsthand experience. McKee, my former husband, and I managed to prolong the Sixties well into the Eighties by taking what we call an early retirement. We hiked, rafted, and skied the American West. Quite the time except for funds in a permanent frown. One winter when legal tender was of particular premium, we subsisted off a pantry of whole wheat flour, oil, yeast, beans, alfalfa seeds, and coffee. I sprouted the alfalfa and made loaf after loaf of fragrant bread. McKee even gathered quite the following for his chile beans. We stayed healthy even as we learned what it means to live at points distant from the land of milk and honey. Rather instructive for a couple of baby boomer, hipster types.

Sprouts are easy and, as aspiring hippie chicks knew way back when, they are living food. So if you need a bit of flower power, grow some sprouts on your kitchen counter. Soak wheat berries, alfalfa seeds, lentils, or mung beans in a wide mouth jar overnight. Secure a piece of screen to the top with a canning band and rinse twice daily until you like the look of things. Sprouts store nicely in the refrigerator for a few days.

Spice Up Your Kitchen Life—

Experimenting with various spices is like opening a door onto a new world. If you need inspiration, check out the spices and herbs in the Mexican food you like, or the Thai or Indian. Then try your own hand—looking for ways to use freshly ground spices and fresh herbs—all the while appreciating our place at a point and time on the American culinary map when fusion cooking is getting especially interesting. Whether you're working with star anise, whole nutmegs, tiny outrageously hot Thai chiles, cardamom pods, or whole allspice or coriander, you'll discover exotic smells and sights and sounds right within the walls of your hippie kitchen.

On Measuring Spices—

Start moderately with a pinch of whatever spice you're working with and see what you think. Instead of dutifully measuring out what someone else prescribes, this is the way to become a cook in your own right. If pinches are too intimidating and you simply must measure, go for half or quarter teaspoon increments at a time. As have everyday people around the world for centuries, you'll soon find your rhythm. But don't take my word for it. Here's what Lynne Rossetto Kasper—host of National Public Radio's Splendid Table—and Sally Swift wrote in their book, *How to Eat Supper*: "An easy way of bettering your lot in the kitchen is to skip the measuring spoons and train yourself to do it by sight. It's simple. Every time a recipe calls for one teaspoon of anything, measure it into a measuring spoon, then plop it into the palm of your hand. We promise, a couple of recipes in, you will know quarters, halves, and wholes by sight."

Tofu Rocker

This one's for Matt Loggins, a dude who isn't square, but who doesn't like Sixties songs much except for "Grateful Dead stuff." And for his daughter, Shellsea, who loves tofu and plays a mean electric guitar with her drummer brother, Cal. And for wife and mother, Michelle, who keeps the family's bubble in the middle. Michelle's a Southern California fox as well, but Garrison Keillor's line still comes to mind about their Upland home: "where the women are strong, the men are good looking, and the children are above average."

Recipe Note

Flash cook some onion on high until soft (page 45) and add leftover baked spaghetti squash. Then a chop of fresh tomatoes, black beans, and kale. Cubed tofu gently folded in makes this so pretty. Grated parmesan finishes Tofu Rocker along with the usual suspects: pepper, salt, vinegar, and oil. At least it does except for the all important buttered toast.

On Onions—

The chore of chopping a fresh onion can seem daunting if you've not done it before or simply gotten out of the habit. There's all that crying business, plus the mess. That's why I very often leave the onion out. It's a pain. I'm in a hurry. What happened recently, though, is that I flash cooked a dice of onion to start a warm salad in more water than I intended.

"Serendipity," I thought. "I'm thirsty so I'll just pour off some of the water and have a cuppa." Wow. You wouldn't believe it. Way sweet and flavorful that warm onion broth was. I've tasted court bouillon before with carrot, onion, and celery—and found it something to write home about. But I always gave carrots the credit. Now I'm hip to onions, as you will be if you try a sip of broth some time. Best of all, these days I'm slicing up an onion because I know from my own experience that it will lend an irresistible flavor to whatever I'm cooking—not because a formulaic recipe calls for "one-half cup chopped..."

On Chopping Hearty Greens—

Since all hearty greens, even curly kale, cook down quite a bit, you'll have a vast mound on the cutting board to start with. But don't get all wigged out. Just corral your critters and make several horizontal cuts through the works. With that done, a vertical chop renders relatively reasonable pieces that won't dangle off spoons and chopsticks. If the horizontal and vertical cuts don't seem to render up polite enough pieces, never fear. Just take your knife into the pile and chop willy nilly, until the greens are as tame as aging hipsters.

On Kale & Her Dark Green Leafy Sisters—

There are all kinds of greens available. Swiss chard, bok choy, dandelion, spinach, mustard, collard, and even nettles. Plenty to keep you from getting in a rut unless you're like me and have eyes mainly for kale. I'll eat spinach, but it's a pain to clean field spinach and in my own garden it hasn't done that well so far. Kale, on the other hand, keeps its curly prettiness when you flash cook it (page 45). You can also grow kale all winter long here in Portland. That's why try as I might to branch out, I keep coming back to good old kale.

On Greens & Their Stems—

To remove the stems from mature kale and chard, fold the leaves in half and slice off the thick parts.

Then you can either add the chopped stems to the pot early so they get a chance to soften before the leaves go in or stash them in the fridge for a pot of soup later on.

Far Out Sage Leaves

There are all kinds of approaches to frying sage leaves. Some cooks dip them in flour or crumbs. Some get fancier with a light batter. Many, like, me just let the leaves come to the fore with a simple fry. Even on the cusp of solstice when fall is about to be eclipsed by winter, my sage plant boasts a clutch of gorgeous leaves merely waiting for a chance to turn into a crispy, far out munchie.

Recipe Note

Pick some nice sized leaves and pinch their stems off. Heat your oil so that when you put a test leaf in it sizzles right up. Do the leaves in batches so they're not crowded and turn them after the few seconds it takes to brown the first side. Drain on something absorbent like a brown paper bag and salt them lightly while they're hot.

Details

I don't rinse my leaves since they're straight from the yard, but if you want to give store bought ones a quick rinse, do dry them well so they won't spit back when they hit the hot oil.

These far out herbaceous leaves blow your mind hot from the pan, but if a lag time can't be helped, keeping them warm in the oven works. That's what I did when I took them to a party Gary and Argelis Lewis had when Gary's parents, Floyd and Alair, were in town visiting. The warm crispy leaves were an usually enticing treat that complemented the excellent dark microbrews we celebrated with that evening.

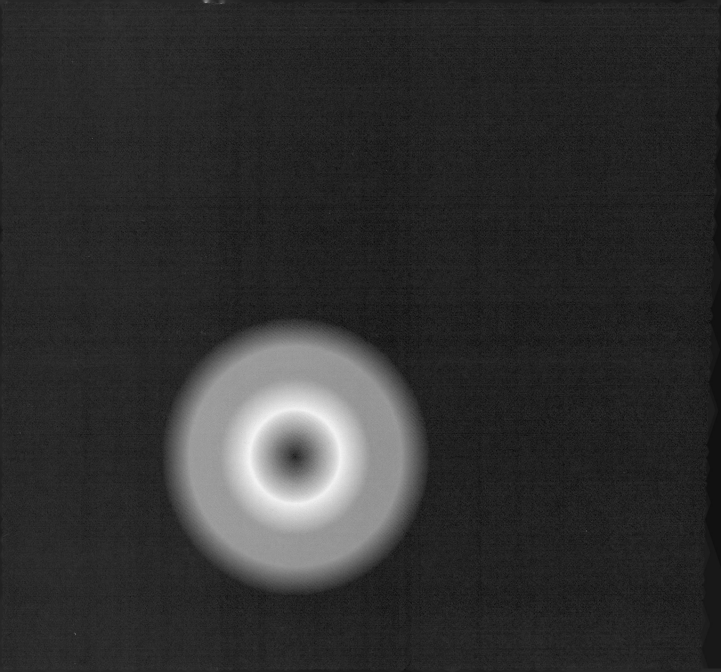

Winter Chow

If there was ever a culture of people who need to hook up with winter, it's mainstream Americans. Us non-siesta-takers. Us independent, highly mobile, multi-taskers who have bought the more-is-better, time-is-money line.

I know the rush-rush vibe has dogged me more than I ever dreamed it would. Like one time in 1982 when I lived up on Second Mesa in Hopiland. You could see forever from the pueblo that day. Out across Navajo where dusty roses and muted purples were a mere suggestion of weavers in pleated velveteen shirts decorated with silver liberty head dimes and buffalo nickels. West and south where the winds came from the San Francisco Peaks, home of the masked gods, the *katsinas*. I, however, saw little of that on this particular day. I was in a hurry doing something, going somewhere.

That's when one of the neighbors piped up and said, "Oh you're such an efficient white lady." He smiled and everyone tee-heed compassionately most likely remembering the times they had been ribbed in their turn. Indeed, joking and teasing is one way tribal people hold a mirror up, helping each other to at least try and keep the bubble in the middle. What a relief to live in that society. To not have to pretend you have it more together than you really do. It was like The Band's "take a load off Fanny" line from Big Pink.

So that's what the gentle but firm nudge did for me that day. Got my attention. Reminded me that kicking back now and then is cool. I can't say I've been all that successful, but the winter kitchen does help bring one back. It's warm in a winter kitchen. You can turn on the oven and bake focaccia. You can smell the fresh yeast bread. You can make soup. You can feel the hardy winter roots in your hands. Hear the rush of steaming water when the broccoli hits the heat. Taste how fun chile and sugar are together in buttery cookies. You can create a very Zennish moment in your winter kitchen—in your hippie kitchen in winter.

Winter Chow

Warm Cauliflower Salad with Fresh Parsley

There's something about winter whites. From snow to clothes to narcissus and cauliflower, winter whites lift us from the darkness and wrap us in an embrace that Janis Joplin was clearly hankering after on her Cheap Thrills album with Big Brother and the Holding Company. Cauliflower does that in this salad, although not in a shy way. Rather from within a veil of fresh cilantro, it dances a sizzling tango up close and personal with the bright red flecks of chile.

Recipe Note

To flash cook your cauliflower, flavor a little water on high heat with turmeric and ground coriander (page 45). Add minced garlic, salt, pepper, and a chop of onion and cauliflower. Cut the heat once the cauli is soft to the tip of your paring knife, but not overdone.

Toss with a mince of fresh parsley and lots of fresh lemon juice. Serve over sharp winter salad greens like endive. Drizzle with walnut oil. Garnish with a few toasted walnut halves. Keep the white theme going and enjoy with a side of steamed quinoa and grated parmesan.

Details

As always choose a commodious pot like a wok or a big skillet. When your cooking vessel is capacious, working with vegetables is so much easier. Just ask any Asian cook.

If you end up with more broth than you want, ladle it out into a mug and enjoy. Then again, you might decide to change tactics and simply serve this as cauliflower soup, mindful as professional chefs are, that the line between warm salads, stews, and soups is a fine one.

On Composed Salads—

Officially, composed salads are creations made from food prepared different ways so that the resulting dish has unique textures and colors.

I wonder, though, if the theory didn't come from professional chefs studying rustic peasant food—food that is so often merely a medley of vegetables, freshly cooked, raw, and leftover set off to great advantage by whatever protein, carbs, fats, and flavorings are handy.

On a Roll with Cauliflower—

I tinkered with the remaining half head of cauliflower, this time using more water to get a soup going, mild leeks instead of onion, and cilantro in place of the flat leaf parsley. The bright flavor and aroma of the cilantro, particularly, made this variation on the theme stand out.

Also because I was out of lemons, a splash of white wine vinegar worked fine. Since I really liked the way the creamy colored quinoa complemented this dish the first time, I stuck with that although instead of serving it on the side again, I swirled the tiny ivory seed grains right into the mix.

On Fresh Cilantro—

Once I realized you didn't have to pick every last leaf away from the smaller stems and could just chop it all up together, my use of fresh cilantro sky-rocketed like Jimi Hendrix's purple haze. It was the same for fresh parsley. The big stems are a bit much and need to go by the way of the compost or the stock pot, but if you can tolerate the smaller ones, it sure makes for shorter work. Minced finely along with the leaves they will have you saying, "Scuse me while I kiss the sky."

On Eating with the Seasons—

It was just a brief few years ago that I trawled the produce sections of mainstream groceries mindlessly, never thinking about where the green peppers for a pizza in January came from. That was back when I thought I couldn't afford local, sustainably grown produce. But the truth was that after I cut back on packaged, processed food—and buying expensive out of season produce—there was enough in the budget to put my money where my heart is. I don't buy fresh peppers in winter anymore, and I've had the pleasure of discovering how vastly better they are when you wait for them and savor them in their time.

Brown University graduate, Louella Hill, agrees. She started the Roots and Shoots program that brought local products into Brown's dining halls in 2004. "There is nothing more beautiful than watching the seasons turn by watching my dinner plate change," Hill told *Home and Garden* magazine in 2007. "My body agrees."

On Steaming Whole Grains—

One part grain to two parts water is a good ratio for steaming grains. Add a little salt and bring your pot to a boil. Then turn to a low simmer and cover until done. Small grains like quinoa take only ten to fifteen minutes, larger ones like brown rice, a half hour to forty-five minutes.

Tangled Up Focaccia

One thing that helped me get a life with focaccia is discovering that the indentations in these round flat discs of bread are not from first rolling the dough out and then poking it with your fingers, but in never picking up the rolling pin in the first place. Indeed, in my hippie mind focaccia is a big, thick tortilla that you round up all nice and then flatten and pat and press into place—without tearing your lovely dough, of course. Besides that, since it's a flat critter, you don't have to worry that it won't get done in the middle like loaves of bread. More, it's done in twenty minutes. Focaccia is right on—and really nothing more than a thick pizza crust without the rim and toppings.

Recipe Note

Mix whole wheat flour with salt and make a well in the middle. Pour in a puddle of warm water and sprinkle your yeast in to dissolve. (Use a teaspoon of yeast for each cup of flour.) Add pink hummus, olive oil, uncooked millet, and more water. Mix first with a spoon and then your clean hands until you've got a nice ball of dough you can knead for a few minutes on a floured board.

Let the dough rise in the bowl you stirred it in until an indentation made with your finger doesn't spring back. Then gently press it down and either go for a second rise or straight to the shaping. Flatten out into a thick round and let rise on an oiled baking tray. Paint with more olive oil. Once it's risen again for a bit and is pretty and puffy, slide it into in a medium oven—and let the smell of freshly baked yeasted dough fill your winter moment.

Details

On how much flour, I usually work with about three cups to a tablespoon (or packet if you don't buy it bulk) of yeast. That will make a nice sized focaccia as well as a pizza crust, something that comes to life simply by rolling out the dough as thin a you like and duding it up with your goodies. Depending on the size pans you use, you might also find you have a small ball of dough leftover for a calzone, those great pizza turnovers. Yum. Just layer your cheese and veggies onto half of this little dandy and then fold the dough over, sealing the edges by pressing them tight.

One trick when you're working with a whole grain dough like this is to press or roll it out as far as it will easily go and then let rest five minutes. When you return to finish up, you'll find it soft and pliable enough to go the distance.

Also if you're going to make pizza and don't want the fun of crunchy millet in your crust, leave it out. It's the same with the pink hummus, but I hope you give at least a small spoonful in your dough a try. You wouldn't need to risk too much your first go round. You wouldn't need to be too hard core. You can use your own common hippie kitchen sense.

The thing is that beans are good food. What's the harm in letting pink hummus bring both some of the liquid you need to the dough as well as a decent hit of protein? Seems right on to *moi*, especially when you put some first rate Crazy Diamond Garlic Butter (page 178) on a warm wedge of focaccia. Then again, my former husband would certainly take issue.

On Former Husbands—

McKee, my ex, loves his pizza. He and I consumed our share through the years, snugged into a booth over a pitcher of beer at Alpine Pizza, a joint that's become institution on Leroux Street in Flagstaff. Yet, MacSpee—as I have taken to calling him most recently— has been so co-opted by the white dough clan that it would take a leap across the Grand Canyon for him to first run some whole wheat rapids never mind scaling the heights of pink hummus and millet. Too bad the turkey always had such little faith in my hippie cooking. Then again, I guess I wasn't the best either. Here's how I got a clue on that score.

It was a few years ago when I was in Northern Arizona and stopped out to see him. Some of the old gang happened by, and we were shooting the breeze when McKee tosses out this remark about how in 1969 a year after we were married, I announced we were becoming vegetarians.

"What?" I thought, stunned at his implication that I issued some sort of edict. "He wasn't into that? He never said a word."

I guess at some level I thought that since he mainly controlled our lives outside the kitchen—and yes dear, in your unassuming way, your hiking boots were planted firmly in the patriarchy—our food decisions were pretty much mine. Also I think I might have concluded that turning vegetarian was such a cool move, that he was as into it as I was. Besides, as I noted, this then-husband of mine didn't give me an inkling that he wasn't a happy hippie veggie.

Sigh. Sometimes I don't know why I've stayed friends with him all these years. Maybe it's because just when I think I've had it, he sends me a letter like the one I got this past May.

It starts with him saying how he was just sitting around spacing out, reading a little nineteenth century history, and listening to Bob Dylan. Turns out that "Tangled Up in Blue" was on —the piece Dylan wrote in 1974 that came out on *Blood on the Tracks.*

"A line from Dylan's song reminds me of you," McKee penned in his old familiar backhand. "'We always did feel the same. We just saw it from a different point of view.'"

On Yeast Dough—

Take this section seriously and you could save some real dough. That's because yeast dough, whether you turn it into loaves, flat focaccia, or pizza pie, is just an affordable mix of flour, water, salt, and yeast—way cheaper than bakery bread. Besides, it's serious play-play.

Play-play on how long you knead it, if in fact you do at all. Play-play on whether you add sugar to the yeast or pink hummus or little crunchy bits of millet or use oil in the dough and for painting the tops. Play-play on how long to let it rise, including overnight if you decide to stir some up on a winter evening before going to bed. Even playing around on whether or not to oil the bowl in which you let the dough rise.

The only critical thing with yeast dough is that the water needs to be baby bottle warm so it can dissolve the yeast but not kill it like hot water will. So test your water with a drop on the inside of your wrist. That way you can make sure your yeasty microorganisms will be able to feed on the natural sugars in the flour and release lots of carbon dioxide to make the dough rise.

What Really Happened—

Someone polished off the last of the pink hummus so I whizzed up some garbanzo beans thawed from a tub I'd frozen the week before (page 74). No tahini around either, so I called it good and named the beanpaste blonde hummus.

Also, I painted the pizza with oil but left the focaccia plain. The former was soft; the latter was crusty.

On the millet it was a different story, since there was a bag from the bulk bins up in the cupboard. But when I poured a handful into the bowl, I realized I'd nabbed the quinoa, not the millet.

The quinoa wasn't quite as crunchy as the millet after the bread was baked, but its seedy nature (technically quinoa is seed not a grain) was uptown and had a pleasing visual presence. Cool when serendipitous mistakes take you in directions you might otherwise not have gone.

Also cool when you make focaccia in the spring, split a wedge for the toaster, layer on ultra thin slices of caramelized goat cheese from Norway (gjetost) and a few local berries, grate on fresh nutmeg, and pour a cup of very dark espresso from just-ground beans.

Those who cruise the web with us have met Iris in the "Cat in the Cheese" blog post.
Known also as Cha-Cha, Iris has a nose for Norske cheese as well.

Dig It Parsnip Bisque

The sweet, earthy parsnip leaps to queendom in this bisque. More, the dish needs no roux or steamed potatoes to become a creamy bowl of comfort food. You'll dig it whether these roots have wintered over in your own garden or not.

Recipe Note

Grate or chop some parsnips, peelings on. Flash cook on high heat in a little water, white wine, and salt (page 45). Purée the works in the blender. (Go directly to page 42 on hot food, blenders, and safety for a do-not-burn-yourself card). Return the snips to the pot and stir in some buttermilk. Once piping hot, ladle into bowls and garnish with minced parsley, paprika, lemon wedges, butter, and black pepper. Count on fresh parsley and lemon to make this soup sexier than you ever dreamed a parsnip could be.

Details

Figure one parsnip for each person. They're tougher to grate than carrots, but using a box grater makes it easy enough. Or just chop them. They're going in the blender anyway.

On the wine, two or three shots for every half dozen parsnips is a good place to start. If you've not cooked with wine, it's instructive to taste before and after this amazingly stellar ingredient has had a chance to mellow into the soup—something it does with a half hour on the stove.

On Bisque—

According to the French cooking bible, Madame E. Saint-Ange's *La Bonne Cuisine*, bisques originally didn't rely on dairy products. Instead these rich, creamy potages or soups acquired their appeal simply from puréed rice and the seafood readily available to the commoners living on the Bay of Biscay.

Somewhere along the line, though—probably as the French peasantry grew affluent enough to afford dairy products—bisques became associated with milk and cream.

Bisque made from puréed rice or other steamed whole grain or potato is a worthy offering that would especially please vegans.

On a Roll with Parsnip Bisque—

As usual when a new winner of a dish appears in the kitchen, we end up wanting to eat it again—wanting to play around with it. But rarely will the same ingredients be on hand for the second round—or the same mood strike the cook.

In this case there was a single parsnip left along with a small rutabaga and turnip. What to do but add even more roots—carrots and onions—along with some outer cabbage leaves left over from grating a batch of Inauguration Slaw 44 (page 172). Also, since with the carrot and onion I was getting over into the land of court bouillon (page 164) some chopped celery stalks and leaves went into the pot as well.

The base for this bisque was plain water without wine, seasoned with salt, pepper, and splash of white vinegar to spike the flavors. On the vinegar, you could use all manner of flavored bottles, but plain white is so affordable and there's enough pizzazz in this soup already. As for the milk, unsweetened soy held the day. A drizzle of olive oil over the top. A mince of chives, mint, parsley that appear outside the kitchen door in late winter. And sweet pecan halves to match the sweet roots for the garnish. The result? A vegan version of parsnip bisque. Dig it?

On Buttermilk—

Buttermilk is what's left over from making butter. Thus it has less fat than sweet milk. At the same time—and this is why it's my bag—it's thick and creamy. My late aunt, Kirsten Johnson Wilson, used to drink buttermilk, as did her mother, Brita Bjornevald Johnson, before her. The old timers knew a good thing when they saw it—mainly because they weren't far removed from the farm and knew all about milking cows and goats and making butter and such.

On Fresh Parsley—

You'll notice that Warm Cauliflower Salad (page 148) and Dig It Parsnip Bisque call for a mince of fresh parsley. They're only two of many ideas in these pages that draw on a hit of this dynamite herb. Parsley, like lemon and lime juice, is really worth more than a passing glance. That's why classic French cooking technique returns to it time and again, in court bouillon, bouquet garni, and mirepoix—each treated on the following pages.

On Court Bouillon—

Court bouillon is essentially seasoned water that French cooks use to poach fish. But as you'll appreciate if you've ever sampled warm broth in which even plain carrots have steeped, court bouillon is so delicious that it's used widely in all kinds of cooking.

Carrots, onion, and parsley—flavorful stems included—are the usuals called for in court bouillon. They are simmered in salted water, with or without white wine, until they've surrendered their flavor. Then they're strained out. Celery is another common element, but some chefs in the nouvelle cuisine tradition shun it for trendier fennel root with its licorice notes.

Another way to monkey with classic court bouillon is to replace the strong onion with milder alliums like shallots or leeks. You can also ditty bop into the land of *bouquet garni* and mirepoix by adding sprigs of thyme, bay leaf, and peppercorns to give an edge to the sweetness the broth picks up from carrots and onions. Add the peppercorns at the end, leaving them in no longer than ten minutes to avoid bitterness, admonishes Madame Saint-Ange.

Note: If this sounds like too much fuss, just taste the broth the next time you cook some onions. Once you discover how immensely sweet and delicious they turn mere water, you'll be a convert and eager to explore the dimensions of carrots and its sisters.

On Mirepoix—

While we're talking classic French technique, we might as well clarify the fancy stuff known as mirepoix. As in court bouillon, aromatic vegetables including onion, carrot, and parsley are used. The difference is that in mirepoix, they are diced and sautéed in fat, not simmered in water. Also, a little thyme and bay leaf are added to the mix.

Madame explains why dicing the onions and carrots is recommended: "It means they will brown evenly, and it helps to extract from the vegetables everything they are capable of offering."

"Oh," HH's keeper, Laura, said. "This is what they call sofritto in Italian cooking. But I'm tired of all that. I want to flash cook."

Laura's into flash cooking because it's an ultrafast way to get very fine food on the table. See page 45 on flash cooking. The lowdown on HH is on page 36.

On Bouquet Garni—

Bouquet garni is yet another way French cooks ensure that their broths are flavorful enough to make people want to bogart the soup tureen. What's nice about this technique is that you take full advantage of the flavor in the parsley stems, and there's no mess from having to chop the herbs. You also wind up with a clear broth, and tying up a bouquet garni is something even the youngest cooks can get in on.

Bind three or four sprigs of parsley and fold them over a sprig of thyme and half a bay leaf. The picture shows how it looks before you fold the fronds back over to make for a tidier bundle secured by some kitchen twine. Once you've done that, drop it in whatever broth you're developing. Not to be missed, of course, is the old world fragrance of the thyme.

I like to leave this rustic bouquet of herbs in the water five to ten minutes. Perhaps it could stay longer, but I cling to the old adage on making tea—you want the leaves to brew not stew.

Hot Chile Cookies

Red chile flakes are such an affordable, easy boon to cooking. I use them so much that they sit out on my cutting board by the cinnamon and salt pots. Not surprising that they found their way into these sweets.

Recipe Note

Cut a cube of butter into two cups of whole wheat flour laced with a half cup each: flax meal, wheat germ, and raw sugar. Leaven with two teaspoons of soda. Perk up with a pinch of salt and red chile. Stir in a cup of buttermilk that should yield a ball of semi-sticky dough ready for chilling.

Once the dough's cool enough to hand, roll it out on board dusted with flour. Cut the cookies into wedges, paint with oil, sprinkle with more of your chunky raw sugar and red chile. Bake for ten or so in a medium oven. Cool on racks.

Details

New to cutting butter into a floury mix? Pastry cutters or forks keep the butter cool while you work, but I prefer my clean hands. The goal is to wind up with flattened bits of butter that will turn the cookies in the direction of a flaky pie crust.

Oil to brush on the tops instead of melted butter? It was a necessity call. Butter might have been nice, but I used all I had in the dough.

Cooling cookies on racks keeps the bottoms from getting soggy. Mom taught me that, and the racks pictured were hers.

...tak, Mama

The chile absolutely makes these cookies.

Spice plus sweet.
An equation the Thais understand,
and one the rest of us are cluing into as well.

Neighbor Patrick Earnest is in the savvy camp.

"Who'd a thunk? Red pepper flakes on cookies???"

He dashed off in an email

"Wow...Delish!"

On Whole Wheat Flour in Goodies—

Whole wheat flour, flax meal, and wheat germ in cookies? Hey, there's nothing like a little nutrition with your sweets. It will help you—as the Rolling Stones belted out in Ruby Tuesday—"catch your dreams before they slip away."

Wheat, of course, is only one of the grains we can draw on. If you can't deal with gluten try whizzing up any number of grains like barley, rye, buckwheat, millet, quinoa, or even the much maligned brown rice in your grinder—whether it be a first rate grain grinder or simply the little one you grind your coffee beans in. All's fair game for creative cooks.

Plus you'll discover how amazingly flavorful freshly ground grains are. Simply no contest between those and the stuff that sits around in bags and bins for months. Really and truly.

Afterthought on Sour Power—

I served these cookies with Bosc pears and lime wedges which got me to thinking that the next time I'll try some fresh lime juice in the dough—like instead of the buttermilk, use half lime juice and half sweet milk. Or even experiment with a vegan approach, letting oil stand in for butter, and using half lime juice and half water—or all lime juice.

Inauguration Slaw 44

The establishment never looked so good to hippie types as the day Barack Obama took the oath of office as the forty-fourth President of the United States. Perhaps that's because President Obama has much about him that is not the establishment. We can only hope. Toward that end, here's a simple winter slaw offered in the statesman's honor.

Recipe Note

Grate cabbage, onion, carrots, and jicama. Dress for success with olive oil, champagne vinegar, celery seeds, salt, and red chile.

Details

I used the big holes on the grater for the jicama in order to give it the prominence a luxurious food is due. Luxury, of course, because this root is imported clear from Mexico. Besides, when you shred on the big holes, things aren't quite such a mess.

Hand grating is messy, especially with cabbage. But when you have a big work surface the clean-up's not too bad. Shredding on a hand grater—box graters help the cause since they stand firmly in place while you're working—makes for such nice results. The shreds are thinner, more refined that what I've seen come from machine graters. And for your efforts, you get a big bowl of slaw that will feed the gang for days to come.

On Cooking for the New Economy—

Yes, we can buy processed food in cans and bags at the stores—even fresh vegetables all peeled and cubed for us. But we don't know where or how these vegetables were grown and what decisions were made in the processing and transporting of them. Plus, the fresh flavor's long gone. That's why we want to dose them with more fat, sugar, and salt that our health can stand. All that and it's expensive—10 to 50 percent extra—to pay other people to process and package our food for us. So it's our choice. We can go for convenience and ante up big time, or roll up our sleeves and rediscover the pleasures of slicing and dicing.

On Giving the Counterculture Its Due—

How else to honor the counterculture's early forays into eating well back in the late-Sixties than to praise the creative, free form cooking that emerged from hippie kitchens. True, these early forays might have been so closely woven into drugs, sex, and rock & roll that they weren't too terribly focused—thus roundly condemned by the mainstream. But forty years later, here we all are.

On Flavor & Elizabeth David's Deconstruction—

Elizabeth David, the woman who brought Mediterranean cuisine to Great Britain in the 1940s, was hip to eating locally and seasonally decades before the rest of us. Not to say David was beyond human frailty; she did get heavy handed with the wine bottle, behavior that egged on her death. Still, she was such a genius at breaking recipes down to their basics that *Harpers* hired her to write a column.

David's theory was to celebrate food, allowing each ingredient shine. Her rule of thumb in combining foods was to think about how they complemented and enhanced each other. No domination. And nothing that doesn't pull its own weight. That's how she thought about food. My experience is that there's much to recommend her philosophy. Here it is in David's own words:

"You may well find the dish is more pleasing in its primitive form, and then you will know that your recipe was too fanciful. If, on the other hand, the dish seems to lack savour, to be a little bleak and insipid, start building it up again. By the end of this process, you will have discovered what is essential to that dish, what are the extras which enhance it, and at what point it is spoilt by over-elaboration."

~~Writing at the Kitchen Table, The Authorized Biography of Elizabeth David
by Artemis Cooper

Hipster Broccoli with Red Peppers

Wedges of Camembert getting all melty atop this warm holiday salad. The thinking was that the broccoli and red peppers needed something creamy. Then again, to make this vegan, all you'd need as a stand in for the cheese is perhaps a new direction in oil—something interesting oil like toasted sesame—and perhaps a squeeze of fresh orange juice along with some toasted sesame seeds and those plump Medjool dates that come out fresh during the holidays.

Recipe Note

Flash cook a chop of broccoli stems on high heat in a puddle of water (page 45). Toss with a chop of roasted red peppers and olive oil, grace with a squeeze of lemon juice and chopped almonds, toasted or not. Nestle in slices of Camembert.

Details

Chop the broccoli stems bite-sized and get them into the water first since they take longer to soften. The more delicate crowns turn tender in just a few minutes of flash cooking.

The best source for red peppers in the middle of winter would be your own freezer. But if you're like me, your supply of red peppers goes fast. The good news is that a small organic company in Napa, California, markets these in jars. I normally steer a wide course around the spendy, inner aisles of the grocery, but for red peppers my knees grow weak. There's the taste—and then the stunning visuals.

Crazy Diamond Garlic Butter

The chunky sea salt from the bulk bins that you use for a bed into which to mince the garlic for this butter really does shine on like Pink Floyd's crazy, crazy diamonds.

Recipe Note

Mince fresh garlic into a bed of coarse salt. Work this brew into room temperature butter. Store your leftovers in the refrigerator where they keep for weeks.

Details

Discovering how easily garlic cloves release from their husks after you smash the cloves with the broad side of a chef's knife opened up the world of cooking with fresh garlic for me. It's easy. Pry a few cloves from a bulb of garlic. Place them flat side down on your cutting board. Place your chef's knife with its wide blade atop each clove and lean in, pressing down on the clove with a sharp staccato hit to release the husk from the meat. Then either trim the tiny tip root end off or say screw it and start mincing.

Working minced garlic into room temp butter is pretty easy with a stout dinner fork, but if you like—or if the kids are helping—just do it with clean hands, washed while singing the Happy Birthday Song three times (for the requisite fifteen seconds of friction required to send the invisible bug life that cruises with us packing).

Do keep your extra garlic butter stored in the refrigerator. Here's what the Food and Drug Administration says: "Left at room temperature, [garlic] mixes may cause potentially fatal botulism food poisoning." Botulism isn't around as much these days, but remember that story about the grandmother who tasted just one drop of the water from her home canned green beans to see if the jar was good? She was gone by the next morning. There you have it. Garlic butter is so very excellent that I almost always have some made up. But it does insist on our utmost respect.

On Kitchen Karma—

There seem to be two camps: two reactions to measurefree cooking, two responses to this offer of freedom from the tyranny of the formal recipe.

The first comes from old and young hipsters alike, denizens of natural food stores and organic gardens who believe in kitchen karma. It goes something like this:

"Cool. That's how I cook." Or, "Yeah, when I apprenticed for a baker from Sweden, that's what he taught me. No times. No temps. Just heat the oven. Then watch the color of the bread, knock on the crust for the hollow sound, and take it out when it's done."

The second comes from those still hanging out in the mainstream world. Their brows knit. Anxiety marks their voice. They want to get it *right*. They fear that they won't, accustomed as they are to deferring to elite cooking authorities. They have forgotten how to rely on their own common sense and go with the flow. Grown disconnected from the joy of seeing a mistake turn into a discovery—or the shoulder shrug that comes the rare times when something simply doesn't work out. They seem to not realize that simple weekday fare is exceedingly forgiving—and that they too can get some good kitchen karma going.

To this latter crowd, courage and fortitude. This is simple everyday cooking; the same cooking that people around the world have been doing for centuries. Yes, they've refined their techniques over time. But also yes, so can we.

On the reluctance score, consider this: while it's common to resist trying new things and learning new approaches, people who overcome their initial unwillingness often find that they develop sensibilities that are nothing short of empowering.

Extravagant promises for switching from a formulaic to an informed style of cooking, you might say. But truly, cooking with understanding instead of a set of rote instructions can't help but build good karma in the kitchen and beyond.

That's because the art of cooking is freeing and makes you smile like prescriptive steps and measuring never could. As the Moody Blues sang on their Seventh Sojourn album,

Someday I know I'll see you smiling
When you're a free man again.

I often wonder why
Our world has gone so far astray.

Someway I know I'll see you shining
When we're all free men again.

Index

A Measurefree Cookbook Trilogy

Cooking Beyond Measure:
  How to Eat Well without Formal Recipes (2008)

Hippie Kitchen:
  A Measurefree Vegetarian Cookbook (2009)

Grow Your Own:
  From the Garden to the Table
  (forthcoming 2010)

~by Jean Johnson

Jean Johnson is a writer and food historian. She lives in Portland, Oregon, and teaches cooking classes hither and yon. Her blog is at measurefree.com.

"We don't have to be gourmet to eat well."